CREATIVE THERAPY III:
52 MORE
EXERCISES
FOR GROUPS

Jane Dossick & Eugene Shea

Illustrated by Eugene Shea

Professional Resource Press
Sarasota, Florida

Published by Professional Resource Press
(An Imprint of Professional Resource Exchange, Inc.)
Post Office Box 15560
Sarasota, FL 34277-1560

This book was produced in the USA using a patented European binding technology called Otabind. We chose this unique binding because it allows pages to lay flat for photocopying, is stronger than standard bindings for this purpose, and has numerous advantages over spiral-binding (e.g., less chance of damage in shipping, no unsightly spiral marks on photocopies, and a spine you can read when the book is on your bookshelf).

The copy editor for this book was Patricia Hammond, the managing editor was Debra Fink, the production coordinator was Laurie Girsch, and the cover designer was Bill Tabler.

Library of Congress Cataloging-in-Publication Data

Dossick, Jane.
     Creative therapy III : 52 more exercises for groups / Jane Dossick &
Eugene Shea : illustrated by Eugene Shea.
        p. cm.
     Includes bibliographical references.
     ISBN 1-56887-008-6
     1. Group psychotherapy--Problems, exercises, etc. I. Shea,
Eugene. II Title.
     [DNLM: 1. Psychotherapy, Group--methods. 2. Creativeness. WM
430   1995]
RC488.D674   1995
616.89' 152--dc20
DNLM/DLC
for Library of Congress   94-35064
                                                             CIP

For Joanne, Philip, Stephanie, Kimberly, and Stephen

TABLE OF CONTENTS

INTRODUCTION

WHO SHOULD USE THIS BOOK?

Like its predecessors, *Creative Therapy: 52 Exercises for Groups* and *Creative Therapy II: 52 More Exercises for Groups,* this book has been designed as a practical guide to assist psychotherapists, group leaders, and specially trained teachers in mental health facilities, nursing homes, day programs, inpatient psychiatric units, special education programs, and support groups.   It may be used as an adjunct to the psychotherapeutic treatment of such varied problems as Alzheimer's disease, schizophrenia, mental retardation, and depression.

The huge success of *Creative Therapy I* and *II* led to the development of this sequel, which contains 52 new therapeutic exercises complete with illustrations that may be photocopied for group members.   The exercises serve as an avenue to therapeutic discussions of important issues that might not be shared through other techniques.   Additionally, we have received feedback regarding the use of these exercises with the individual treatment of children.   We have learned that children may enjoy the exercises and are consequently less inhibited about sharing fears, concerns, and fantasies.

As we did in the previous two works, this new book explains methods of energizing a group and takes both new and experienced group leaders through the stages for effective implementation of structured exercises.   We have used these kinds of materials successfully in a major New York city long-term care hospital.   We find that these exercises can help group members develop interactive skills, motivate less-verbal individuals to contribute to group discussions, and encourage group cohesiveness.

WHAT IS IN THIS BOOK?

Creative Therapy III: 52 More Excercises for Groups is presented in an uncomplicated fashion so that the exercises will be nonthreatening to group members.   The format allows the leader to refer to directions for each group meeting, and to photocopy the accompanying illustration, which becomes each member's worksheet.   In each exercise, members complete a picture that focuses on a particular theme.   A discussion follows in which the members discuss what their completed pictures reveal about themselves.   Each member is able to look at his or her own illustration and express an initial response that might otherwise have been forgotten.   The illustrations are intentionally simple to encourage participants to express themselves as freely as possible.

HOW DO YOU USE THIS BOOK?

Creative Therapy III: 52 More Excercises for Groups combines the structured expression of art groups with the therapeutic communication of verbal discussion groups.   The worksheet provided with each exercise serves as a springboard to discussion for group members.   Each exercise is accompanied by a step-by-step set of instructions for the group leader.

Group members sit at a table, preferably in a circle. The leader hands out photocopies of the chosen exercises to members at the beginning of the session. The leader should seek to involve members immediately by asking about the picture.

The group leader introduces the theme, describes the exercise according to the instructions that accompany each drawing, and asks for feedback and comments from the group members. This initial discussion should be used to prepare the members for the task that follows.

Next, group members are given a time frame and directed to "fill in" or complete the exercise with their responses. Additional supplies such as crayons, markers, pens, or pencils may be handed out at this time.

It is important to be certain that everyone has a clear understanding of the task. If questions arise, it is recommended that members be encouraged to ask each other to paraphrase the instructions. In this way members become actively involved and discover they can be helpful to one another.

Setting up a time frame is an important aspect of the structured exercise. These projects work best if the group members understand how much time is set aside for drawing, and how much time is for discussion. For example, in a 1-hour group, 20 minutes might be used for explanation and drawing, and 40 minutes for discussion.

These exercises should be nonthreatening. To reduce anxiety, group leaders should explain that content is more important than artistic talent, and that the drawings are used simply to promote discussion. Some members may be resistant to drawing because of self-consciousness or physical limitations. Encouragement is helpful, but too much encouragement may become stressful. An alternative is to avoid adding extra pressure by allowing anxious members to write rather than draw their interpretations.

Group discussion immediately follows the drawing period. The leader should state a few minutes ahead of time when this will take place. Once group discussion begins, all members' comments should then be directed to the group as a whole.

Members are asked to volunteer to discuss their interpretations. The leader becomes a catalyst to promote and encourage verbal interaction and help focus the discussion. As members see one another present and receive feedback, more may volunteer to discuss their work.

WHAT ARE THE BENEFITS?

Projective art tasks introduce ideas that provide encouragement to groups searching for a common theme (Dalley, 1984). In addition, these structured exercises have a variety of other uses: to initiate members into a group process; as a warm-up technique; to help a group work through a particular stage in its development; to enhance group members' abilities to interact and share freely; to focus on a specific group need; and to help reduce group members' anxiety and uncertainty. For example, if used with children, the exercises allow the child to indirectly or directly express important ideas, fantasies, and feelings. Significant information about family members and dynamics are often shared as a result of this approach. It must be understood, however, that these techniques are intended as a tool - as one part of a total approach to meet the goals of a particular group.

Structured exercises are a way of accelerating group interaction. Getting in touch with suppressed emotions helps the group as a whole as well as the individual members. Specific exercises may be chosen to help the group work through a particular problem (Hansen, Warner, & Smith, 1980).

Yalom (1983) describes the use of structured exercises with lower-level, inpatient psychotherapy groups. These groups often consist of members with a limited attention span, fearfulness, and confusion. Structured exercises may help such members express themselves. The use of art or drawing exercises is especially helpful in fostering self-expression. These exercises may also stimulate group interest and provide variety. We believe the exercises in *Creative Therapy III: 52 More Exercises for Groups* are very effective with this type of group.

Structured exercises also help insure that no one dominates and that everyone has an opportunity to speak. A balance of verbal input is created. Monopolistic members must develop self-control to allow other members to have their turns. Shy or nonverbal members profit from the required participation, such as described by Levin and Kurtz (1974). These authors studied the effects of structured exercises in human relations groups and concluded that the inactive person benefits from a change in behavioral expectations. Greater opportunity for participation generates more ego-involvement, self-perceived personality changes, and increased group unity.

How does group therapy help group members? Feedback from one's peers, if properly channeled, can be a potent therapeutic force, promoting qualitative changes in self-expression, growth toward self-actualization, and changes in interpersonal behavior.

In his classic work on group psychotherapy, Yalom identifies key curative factors associated with the group process. We believe that many of the exercises included in *Creative Therapy III: 52 More Exercises for Groups* facilitate the curative process. Generally, the exercises encourage sharing and development of trust among group members. The drawings illustrate common fears and anxieties and allow group members to see how they share many of the same concerns. Through the use of the illustrations, members are encouraged to support each other in finding solutions to problems and learning to support each other's needs. Skilled therapists will use the exercises strategically to support the development of other curative factors within the group.

WHAT ARE THE LIMITATIONS OF THESE EXERCISES?

Through experience, we have found these exercises and materials to be of great value. It is important, however, to realize the limitations of their use. As we have said, these exercises are to be used as a springboard to discussion and as an adjunct to other therapies.

Yalom (1985) describes possible negative effects structured exercises can have on groups. He suggests, for example, that they can create an atmosphere where critical stages of group interaction may be passed over. Structured exercises may also plunge the group members into sharing significant negative and positive feelings too quickly. In addition, the group leader may be too heavily relied upon by the members. This dissipates a group's potential effectiveness as a therapeutic agent.

The Lieberman, Yalom, and Miles encounter group project (1973) studied how structured exercises influence groups. The leaders who used relatively large numbers of structured exercises with their groups were often more popular with group members. However, group members were found to have a significantly lower outcome level than members participating in groups using fewer structured exercises.

There must be a balance to the use of structured exercises. The degree to which they should be used must be carefully weighed by the group leader; otherwise the leader runs the risk of reducing the group's potential and infantilizing the members. Some factors that determine the amount and type of structuring to be employed are the type of group, member characteristics, and the leaders' theoretical orientation (M. S. Corey & G. Corey, 1987).

Additionally, the group leader should keep in mind three of the considerations noted by Pfeiffer and Jones (1983). First, structured exercises should address the specific goals and purposes of the group. The leader should choose exercises directed at interests, concerns, or problems of individual members or of the group as a whole. Second, a more than casual understanding of the members is important, because revelation and exploration of fantasy can be threatening and anxiety provoking. Less-threatening exercises are recommended for groups with anxious or guarded members to promote openness rather than defensiveness. Third, different issues surface at various stages of group development. Groups will function best when the level of feedback expected corresponds to the developmental stage of the group. In early stages of group development, exercises that focus on openness and building trust are more appropriate. Exercises that focus on critical feedback and appraisal will be more successful in the later stages of group development.

CONCLUSION

Creative Therapy III: 52 More Exercises for Groups should offer rewarding experiences for both group leaders and group members. The structured exercises in this book make it easier for group members to focus ideas, feelings, and experiences related to the topic of discussion. Members further benefit from revealing themselves, exchanging feedback, and supporting one another emotionally.

The purpose of this book, however, is first and foremost to help group leaders, therapists, and teachers conduct their groups by providing a framework for successful group experiences. Through the use of specific suggestions, we describe the procedures necessary for group leaders to handle the widest variety of group therapy applications.

In addition, the use of these exercises may also help to alert group leaders to issues for further exploration in individual counseling or other group therapies. Although designed primarily for groups, with slight modification these exercises can be used in individual treatment. In particular, they may be most helpful for children.

REFERENCES

Corey, M. S., & Corey, G. (1987). *Groups: Process & Practice* (3rd ed.). Monterey, CA: Brooks/Cole.

Dalley, T. (1984). *Art as Therapy: An Introduction to the Use of Art as a Therapeutic Technique*. New York: Tavistock.

Hansen, J. C., Warner, R. W., & Smith, E. J. (1980). *Group Counseling: Theory and Process* (2nd. ed.). Chicago: Rand McNally.

Levin, E. N., & Kurtz, R. R. (1974). Structured and non structured human relations training. *Journal of Counseling Psychology, 21,* 526-531.

Lieberman, M. A., Yalom, I. D., & Miles, M. B. (1973). *Encounter Groups: First Facts*. New York: Basic Books.

Pfeiffer, J. W., & Jones, J. E. (1983). *A Handbook of Structured Experiences for Human Relations Training: Reference Guide to Handbooks and Annuals*. San Diego: University Associates.

Shulman, L. (1979). *The Skills of Helping Individuals and Groups*. Itasca, IL: F. E. Peacock.

Yalom, I. D. (1983). *Inpatient Group Psychotherapy*. New York: Basic Books.

Yalom, I. D. (1985). *The Theory and Practice of Group Psychotherapy* (3rd ed.). New York: Basic Books.

CREATIVE THERAPY III:
52 MORE
EXERCISES
FOR GROUPS

Exercise 1

THE ICE BREAKER

Purpose:

1. To promote an atmosphere for group interaction.
2. To promote group identity and cohesion.

Materials:

One photocopy of the illustration for each member; pencils, pens, markers, or crayons.

Description:

A. The leader introduces the phrase, "Breaking the Ice." This is discussed by the group members and related to the experience of the members' initial participation in the group.
B. As the materials are distributed, the leader describes this exercise as a way for members to ask each other questions in order to get to know one another better.
C. On the illustrated "ice cube" being held, members are asked to write either a question they want to ask a fellow member, or something they wish to know about the future of the group.
D. The group leader collects the illustrations and places them on a pile or in a container that serves as an "ice bucket."

Group Discussion:

Members take turns picking out a question from the "ice bucket." Each written question becomes the focus of a short discussion, with the leader encouraging as many members as possible to participate. As the questions are posed, members may have comments and other questions to add to the discussion.

This exercise may be a useful tool for members to get to know one another. It is therefore practical with any group type during the early stages of development.

Exercise 1

Exercise 2

GETTING OFF THE GROUND

Purpose:

  1. To recognize universal concerns about the group experience.
  2. To incorporate individual needs into the group process.
  3. To develop insight into group dynamics.

Materials:

One photocopy of the illustration for each member; pencils, pens, markers, or crayons.

Description:

  A. The group leader begins a discussion about everyone's initial reaction to being a participant in a group. The members are reassured that it is common for people to have concerns when beginning a group.
  B. The group leader shows the members the illustration. The group members are encouraged to relate the picture of the balloon to their concerns about getting the group "off the ground."
  C. In the space provided on each separate balloon drawing, the group leader writes a few words that summarize the issues or concerns brought up by group members.
  D. The balloon drawings are then distributed at random to the group members. Each member is asked to write his or her response to the topic received. They do not have to sign their names.
  E. The completed illustrations are collected by the leader.

Group Discussion:

The group leader reads the comments about the group process out loud. The group members are encouraged to explore whether or not any of the recommendations could become practical guidelines for running the group in the future.

This exercise may help group members explore their expectations about the group process, and is an opportunity for input into the group experience.

This exercise may be useful during the earliest stages of group development and is a way for members to become acquainted with each other.

Exercise 3

CAPTURED ON CANVAS

Purpose:

    1. To reveal self-image through fantasy.
    2. To allow participants to receive feedback in a nonthreatening way.

Materials:

    One photocopy of the illustration for each member; pencils, pens, markers, or crayons.

Description:

    A. The group leader introduces the idea that being the subject of a painting might reveal a great deal about the image we think we project to others.
    B. Members are given the illustration of the blank canvas.
    C. On the blank canvas, the leader asks members to draw a scene which they think best represents them.
    D. In addition, the picture may include others from either the group or their own lives.

Group Discussion:

    Each member shares his or her "canvas." They explore the reasons they have illustrated the particular scene. They also explain why they may have chosen to include any other people in the scene with them.
    Members help them examine the significance of each other's scene. Similarities and differences are explored.
    Group members often add constructively to the discussion, commenting on the personal strengths and qualities of each member.
    This exercise should be used by groups in which members have developed a degree of trust and are well acquainted with one another.

Exercise 4

CLOWNING AROUND

Purpose:

    1. To facilitate a common bond between members.
    2. To encourage interpersonal learning through the sharing of constructive responses to negative situations.

Materials:

    One photocopy of the illustration for each member; pencils, pens, markers, or crayons.

Description:

    A. The group begins with a discussion of the idea that at times humor is appropriate to many situations; on the other hand, there are situations when humor may be detrimental.
    B. As the materials are distributed, members discuss the concept of how humor in groups can sometimes be either a positive or negative force within the group process.
    C. Alongside the picture of the clown with "YES" written on it, members are asked to write or draw a situation in the group when humor is suitable or desirable.
    D. Alongside the picture of the clown with "NO" written on it, members are asked to write or draw a situation in the group when humor is not appropriate.

Group Discussion:

    Members describe their drawings. The leader encourages feedback from group members as each illustration is presented. It is important to focus on feelings members have about some negative effects of humor in the group situation.

    This exercise gives members an opportunity to offer constructive ways of dealing with situations that may arise during the group process, and to share viewpoints.

    This exercise is effective with group members that are well acquainted with each other, in the middle to later stages of group development.

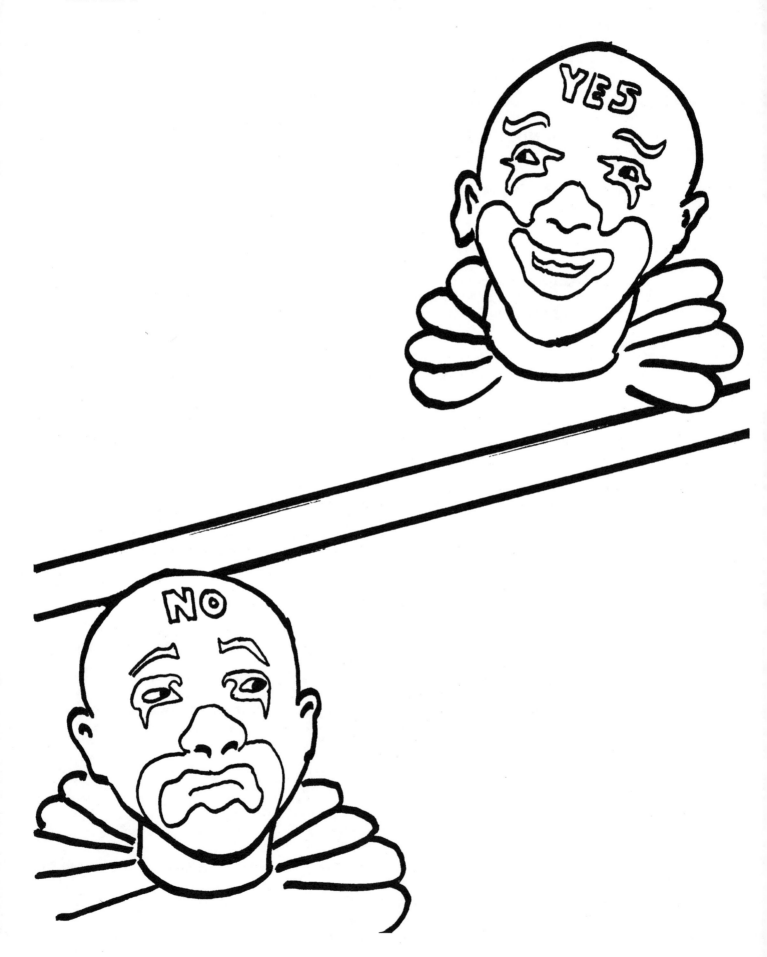

Exercise 5

AT YOUR LEISURE

Purpose:

    1. To express viewpoints and perspectives about leisure-time activities.
    2. To explore new ways to use free time.

Materials:

One photocopy of the illustration for each member; pencils, pens, markers, or crayons.

Description:

    A. The leader asks the members to share thoughts about the meaning of leisure time.
    B. The materials are distributed and members describe how the illustration relates to their own thoughts and feelings about leisure time.
    C. In the space provided, members illustrate the activities that they pursue in their spare time.

Group Discussion:

Members share their illustration and describe in detail what they do in their leisure time. Members are asked to interpret each other's choices and their significance. Similarities and differences are focused on.

Suggestions for other activities, and ways to enhance what they are already doing in their leisure time, are explored.

Because this exercise is relatively nonthreatening, it is effective with all group types, in all stages of development.

Exercise 5

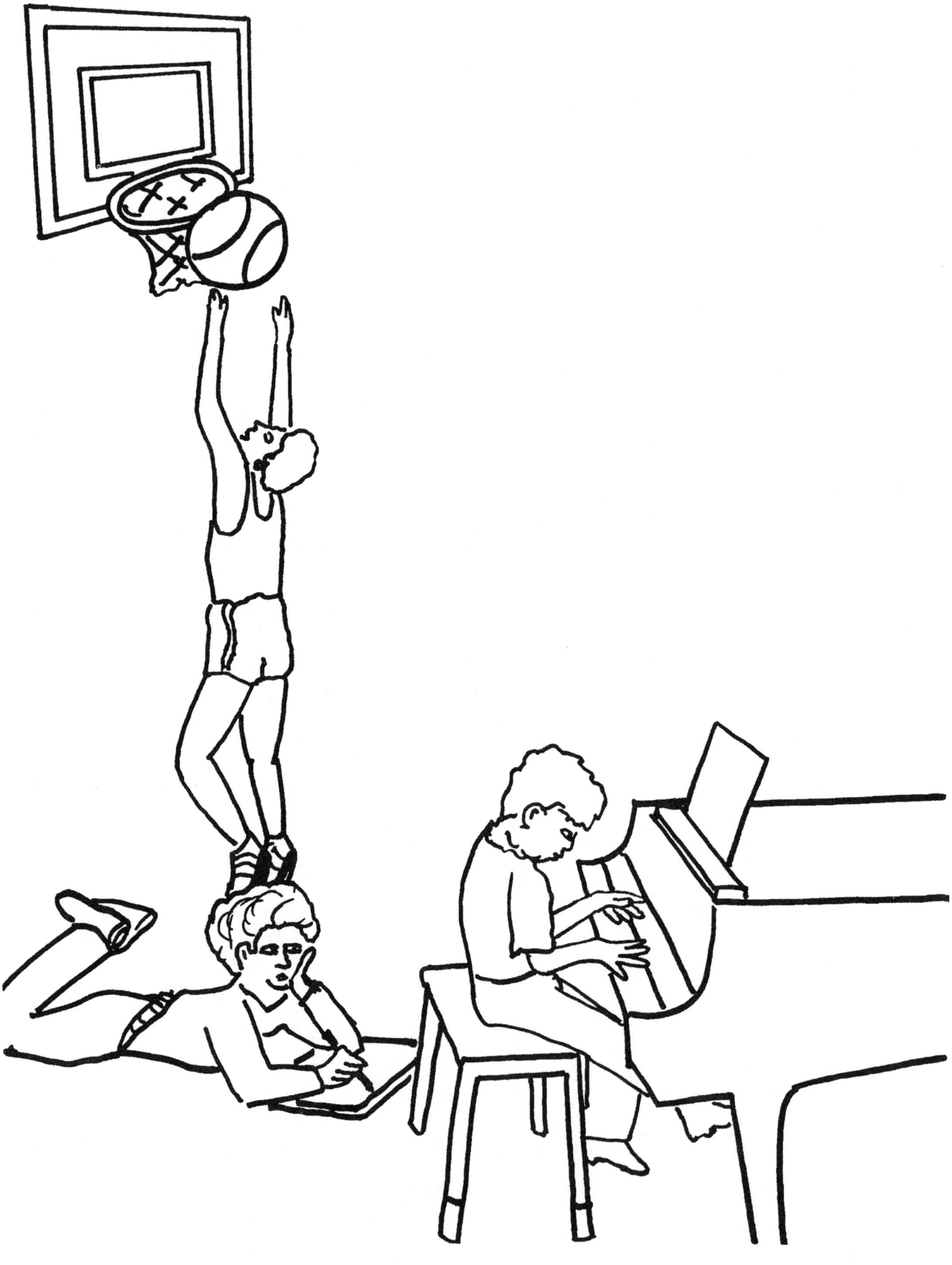

Exercise 6

THE CLASSROOM

Purpose:

    1. To create a supportive atmosphere.
    2. To share memories and compare experiences.

Materials:

    One photocopy of the illustration for each member; pencils, pens, markers, or crayons.

Description:

    A. The group leader distributes the materials and briefly discusses the illustration of an empty classroom. The leader asks the members to think back to the time when they were still in school.
    B. Members are asked to draw or write about one or more significant events involving friends, teachers, parents, the school principal, or anyone else they can remember from those days.
    C. These can be positive, negative, or any other noteworthy experiences.

Group Discussion:

    The members share their illustrations. The leader encourages members to ask questions about the experiences recalled and why they were chosen. Common experiences will emerge and should be focused on. The leader helps members explore each other's feelings about the content depicted. Members are asked if they would relive the same experience again, regardless of the outcome.

    Because of the open-ended nature of this exercise, it is effective with all group types, at all stages of development.

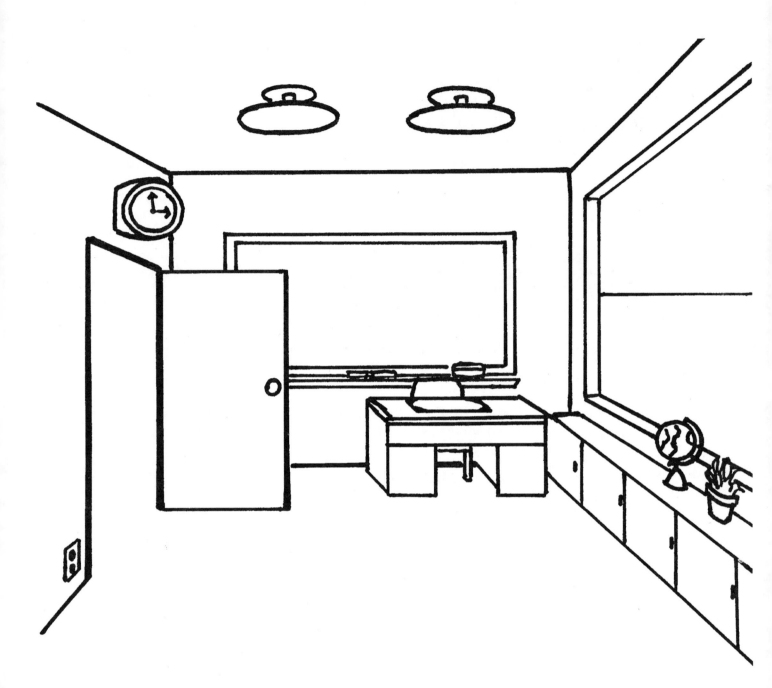

Exercise 7

MY PARADE

Purpose:

1. To share memories and compare experiences.
2. To develop a group climate for interaction.
3. To use reminiscence as a learning experience.

Materials:

One photocopy of the illustration for each member; pencils, pens, markers, or crayons.

Description:

A. The leader engages the members in a brief discussion of how positive memories of experiences in our lives influence how we feel now.
B. As the materials are distributed, the group leader initiates a discussion about how one's life can be thought of as a "parade." The whimsical idea of the high points of one's life being represented as floats, balloons, and banners in a parade is introduced.
C. Members are asked to illustrate some of the high points in their lives by drawing or writing on the spaces provided.

Group Discussion:

Members share their illustrations. They describe the high points they have illustrated. Members are encouraged to ask each other questions about these experiences and expand upon the impact of these events in their lives.

This exercise is effective with virtually all group types. It is a particularly useful method by which members in newly formed groups can become better acquainted.

Exercise 7

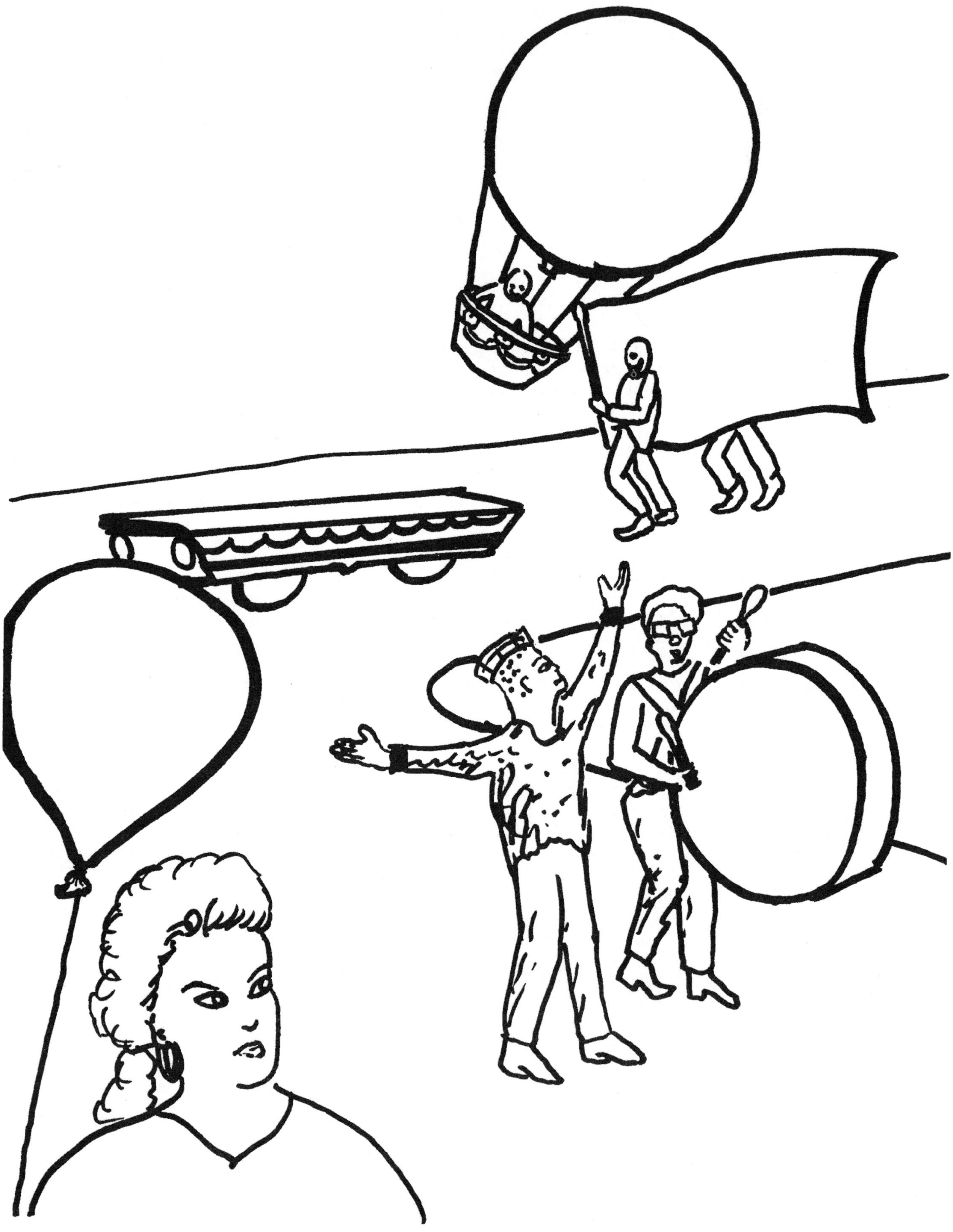

Exercise 8

SPECIAL INVITATION

Purpose:

1. To be responsive to each other's needs.
2. To promote group identity and cohesion.

Materials:

One photocopy of the illustration for each member; pencils, pens, markers, or crayons. One hat. Group members' names written on individual pieces of paper.

Description:

A. The group members are asked to describe how it feels to receive invitations to go for a cup of coffee, to go for a meal, to go for a visit with someone, or to attend a special event such as a party.
B. The materials are distributed. At random, members draw each other's names out of the hat.
C. In the space provided on the illustrated invitation, members are asked to write the name of the person whose name they have chosen from the hat.
D. They are asked to illustrate a place, an event, or an experience they would like to share with that person.
E. After completing the invitations, the members are asked to give each one to the person they have chosen to invite.

Group Discussion:

Each member describes the invitation they have received. The leader invites them to comment on why they think the event was chosen for them. The member who sent the invitation is asked to describe the reason for his or her choice. The group is encouraged to interpret each other's choices, and their significance.

This exercise gives the group an opportunity to express positive feelings about one another and is effective with any group type at all stages of development.

THE VACATION

Purpose:

    1. To explore fantasies in order to promote heightened awareness of self and others.
    2. To explore what qualities attract one person to another.

Materials:

    One photocopy of the illustration for each member; pencils, pens, markers, or crayons.

Description:

    A. The leader begins the exercise by distributing the materials and asking members how they would feel about taking a trip somewhere with a companion.
    B. Members are asked to decide where they would like to visit. The leader asks them to write or draw this on the space within the illustrated travel poster.
    C. In the depicted doorway, members draw a traveling companion. This may be a group member or anyone else.
    D. In the depicted suitcase, members draw some of the items they would take with them to their destination.

Group Discussion:

    Members share their illustrations. The leader asks each member to describe their destination, items taken along, and who they chose to be their traveling companion. The reasons for these choices are examined. The group is engaged in a discussion of what the choice of destination, items taken along, and traveling companion reveal about each member.
    It is interesting to explore the personal qualities of the chosen traveling companion. Is it someone the group member is close to, or would like to be close to?
    The self-revelation involved in this exercise is relatively nonthreatening. This makes it appropriate for groups of any type, in the early stages of group development.

Exercise 10

WHEEL OF FORTUNE

Purpose:

1. To explore fantasies as an expression of one's needs.
2. To promote an atmosphere for self-disclosure.

Materials:

One photocopy of the illustration for each member; pencils, pens, markers, or crayons. In addition: one hat, and six small pieces of paper, numbered consecutively 1 to 6.

Description:

A. The leader begins the discussion by encouraging the group to talk about the symbolism of a "wheel of fortune."
B. As the materials are distributed, this discussion is related to the depicted wheel of fortune. Members are asked to make note of the different categories in each spoke of the wheel. The "wild card" can be any category the member chooses.
C. The group leader holds up the hat and asks each member to pick a number out of the hat.
D. Members are asked to match their number to the illustrated categories on the wheel, and write or draw in the space provided whatever their category suggests to them.

Group Discussion:

The group leader asks each member to share what he or she has written or drawn. The member is asked to explain his or her choices. Other members are invited to comment on the significance of these choices. Where appropriate, members are encouraged to provide advice and suggestions about how some of these "fortunes" may be achieved.

This exercise is useful with any group type in the early stages of development.

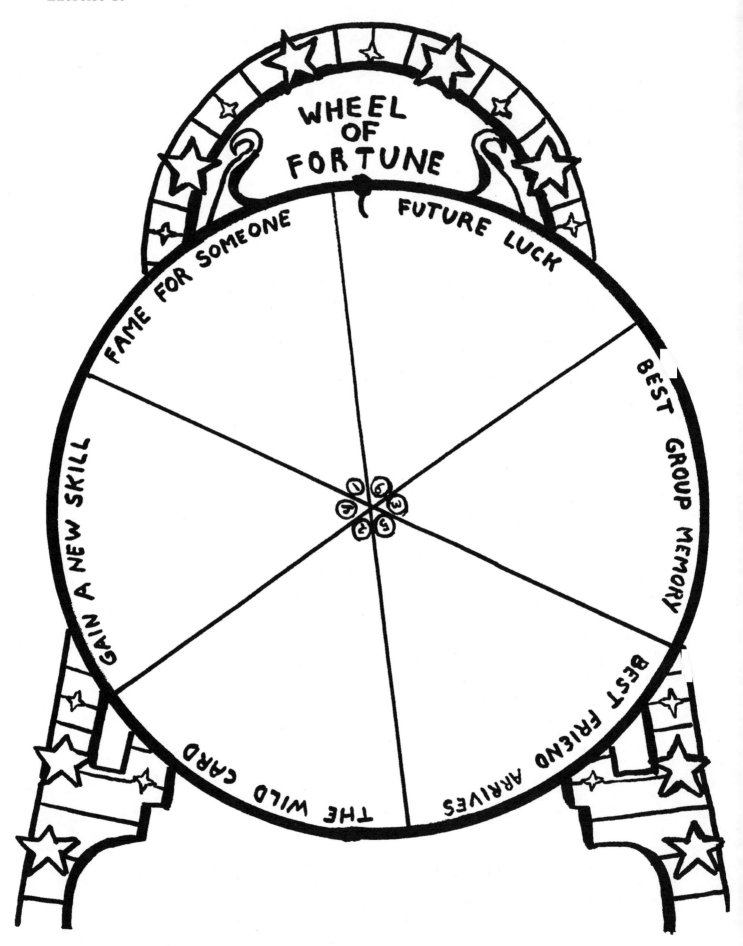

Exercise 11

THE MAGIC CARPET

Purpose:

    1. To explore fantasy in order to promote heightened awareness of self.
    2. To share personal information in a nonthreatening way.

Materials:

One copy of the illustration for each member; pencils, pens, markers, or crayons.

Description:

    A. The group leader introduces the idea of using one's imagination to travel anywhere we might wish to go.
    B. The concept of an imaginary flying carpet is introduced as the materials are distributed.
    C. The group members are asked to draw themselves on the magic carpet, and in the sky below, the place they would like to go. They may also illustrate someone they would like to travel with.

Group Discussion:

Each member shares his or her drawing. The group leader encourages the members to explore the reasons they chose their specific destination. If depicted, they are asked to describe why they chose their particular traveling companion.

Group members are invited to speculate on the experiences they might have when they arrived at their selected destination.

Group members are asked to explore some of the differences between this imaginary place and the place they live in now.

This exercise is both entertaining and revealing. It is useful during the early stages of group development, with any group type.

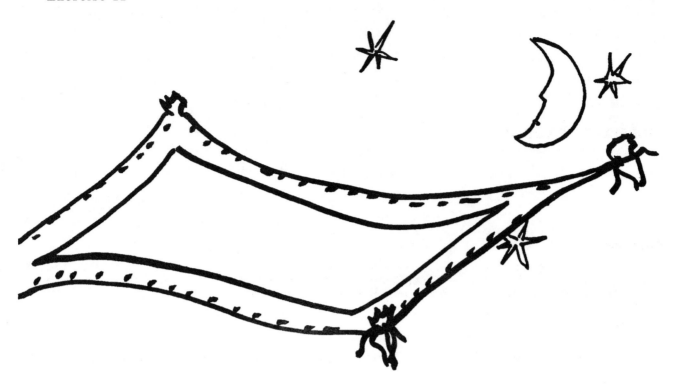

Exercise 12

FEELING LEFT OUT

Purpose:

1. To understand the significance of acceptance and rejection.
2. To gain insight about interpersonal behavior.

Materials:

One photocopy of the illustration for each member; pencils, pens, markers, or crayons.

Description:

A. The group leader introduces the idea of what it feels like to be left out or not included in group activities. The group members are asked to describe any experiences they may have had of being left out of some activity or situation.
B. Materials are distributed. Members are asked to describe how the illustrated picture relates to the theme.
C. Members are asked to draw a situation in the space provided which makes the depicted child in the illustration feel left out.

Group Discussion:

Group members are asked to describe the situation which they have drawn. The group leader raises the question of whether or not the depicted experience ever really happened to the group member. In addition, group members are asked to reveal if they have ever done something to make others feel left out.

Though actual situations and how they were dealt with may vary, the leader should help members concentrate on feelings shared in common.

Often, this exercise leads members to reveal unknown issues and concerns about their group experience.

This exercise is effective for any group beyond the initial stage of development.

Exercise 12

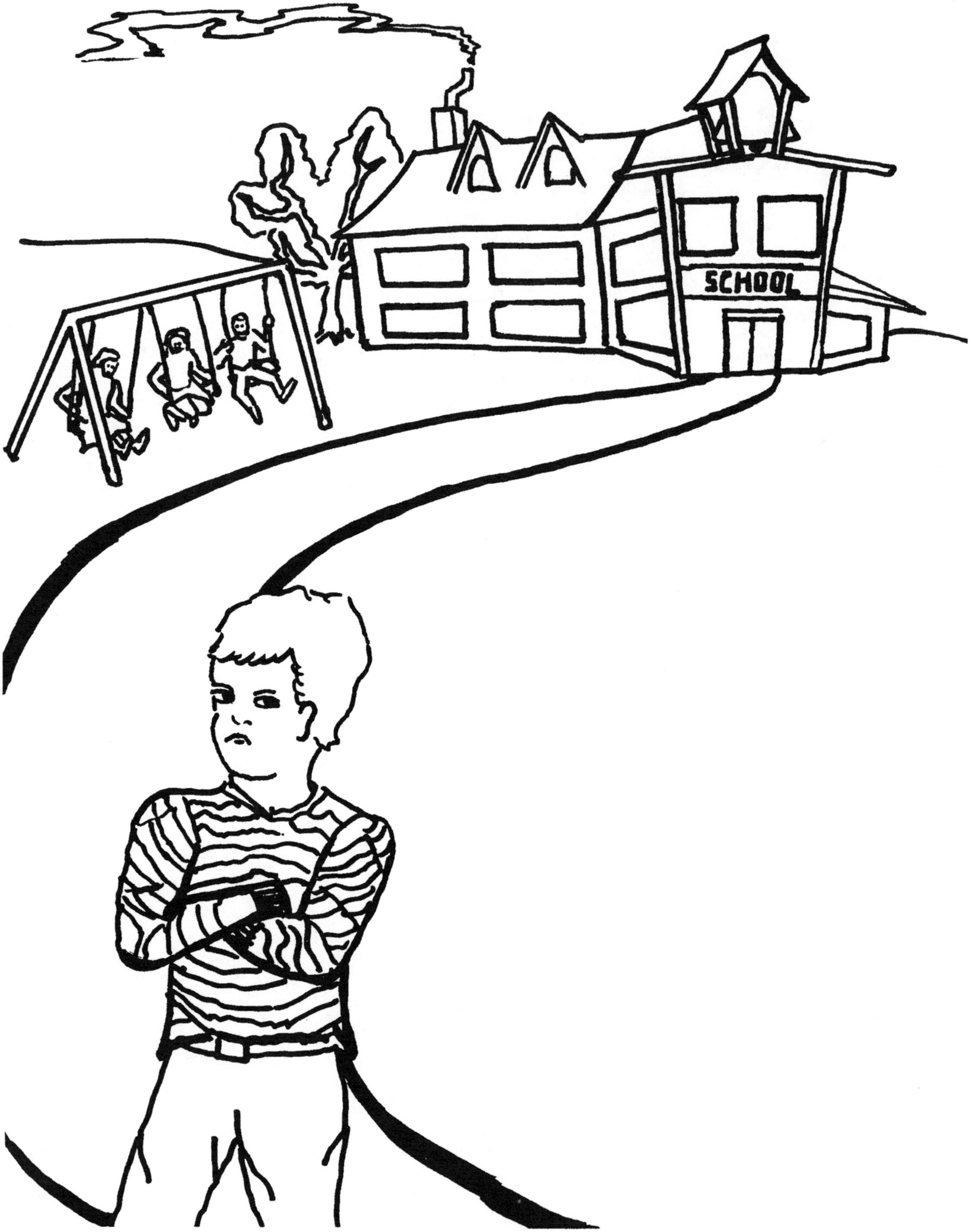

Exercise 13

THE CLEAN SWEEP

Purpose:

    1. To recognize that many problems are universal.
    2. To encourage empathy through sharing negative aspects of one's life.

Materials:

One photocopy of the illustration for each member; pencils, pens, markers, or crayons.

Description:

    A. The group leader asks if any of the group members have ever wished they had the power to easily remove something negative from their lives.
    B. While handing out the materials, the leader asks members to relate this theme to the concept of sweeping something away with a broom.
    C. In the space provided, the leader asks members to imagine sweeping something negative from their lives. This could be anything, including an object, a person, a place, a feeling, or a memory.

Group Discussion:

Members describe the negative element of their lives they are sweeping away. The leader helps the group to identify feelings and common themes.

Members are encouraged to provide constructive advice and suggestions about how best to adjust to the described negative element.

This exercise works well with almost any group type in any stage of development because of its wide range of acceptable responses (person, object, place, feeling, or memory). In addition, it may be useful in acquainting new members with one another in the early stage of group development.

Exercise 14

THE DAY DREAM

Purpose:

 1. To develop self-awareness through fantasy.
 2. To identify potential treatment goals.

Materials:

 One photocopy of the illustration; pencils, pens, markers, or crayons.

Description:

 A. The group leader initiates a brief discussion of the significance of fantasy and daydreams in members' lives.
 B. The materials are distributed.
 C. The group members are encouraged to share initial reactions about how the illustration relates to the theme of fantasy and daydreams.
 D. Members are asked to illustrate a fantasy or daydream in the space provided.

Group Discussion:

 Group members are asked to describe their drawings to the other members. The significance of the fantasy/daydream, and how it relates to the members' real lives is explored. The group leader helps the members focus on whether or not this fantasy could be a realistic goal.

 This exercise can be interpreted on many levels. It may stimulate an increased awareness of the members' concerns and fears as they relate to self-perception. It may also be useful because it provides a nonthreatening way to divulge personal information, wishes, and desires.

 This exercise is appropriate in the early to middle stages of group development, with any group type, as it may be interpreted on many levels.

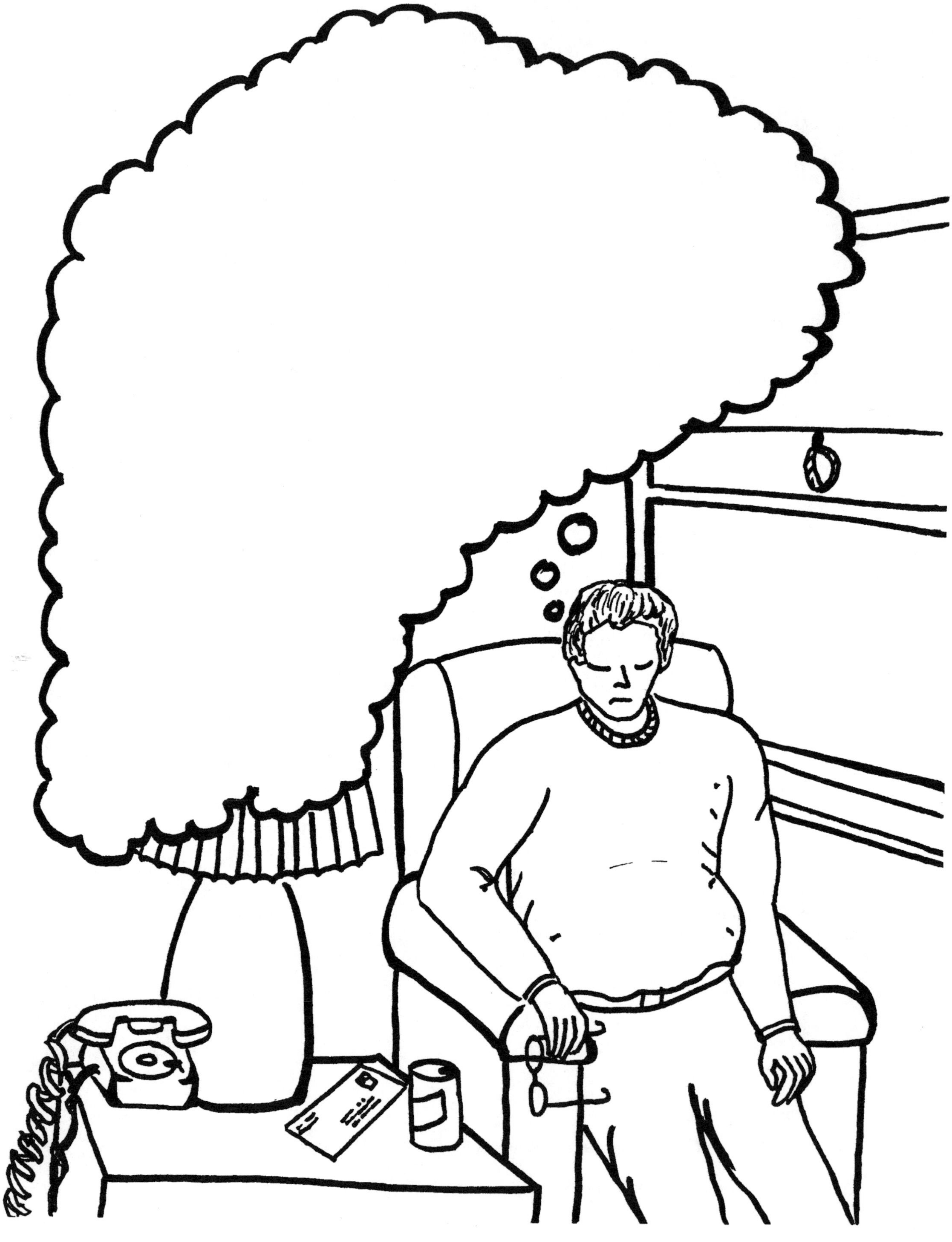

Exercise 15

THE STEPS YOU TAKE

Purpose:

    1. To encourage empathy and insight.
    2. To reassure members that they can help one another.

Materials:

    One photocopy of the illustration for each member; pencils, pens, markers, or crayons.

Description:

    A. The group leader begins a discussion about how members can be supportive and helpful to each other. Group members comment on this and are asked to provide examples.
    B. The materials are distributed. In the picture of the circle labeled "Present Situation," members are asked to write or illustrate a difficult situation or problem in their own lives they would like to improve.
    C. In the picture of the circle marked "Future Goal," members are asked to illustrate or write what they hope to achieve in the future.
    D. The leader collects the sheets and redistributes them to the group at random. On the illustrated stair steps, members are now asked to write or draw the steps they think could be taken to help solve the problem/situation and reach the future goal.

Group Discussion:

    Each member is called upon to share an illustration. They describe the steps they would take to try to solve the depicted problem/situation. The group is encouraged to comment and say whether they agree with the suggested steps. Alternate steps may be suggested. The member whose problem/situation is being described may choose to remain anonymous.
    This exercise may be useful in the early to middle stages of group development, with all group types.

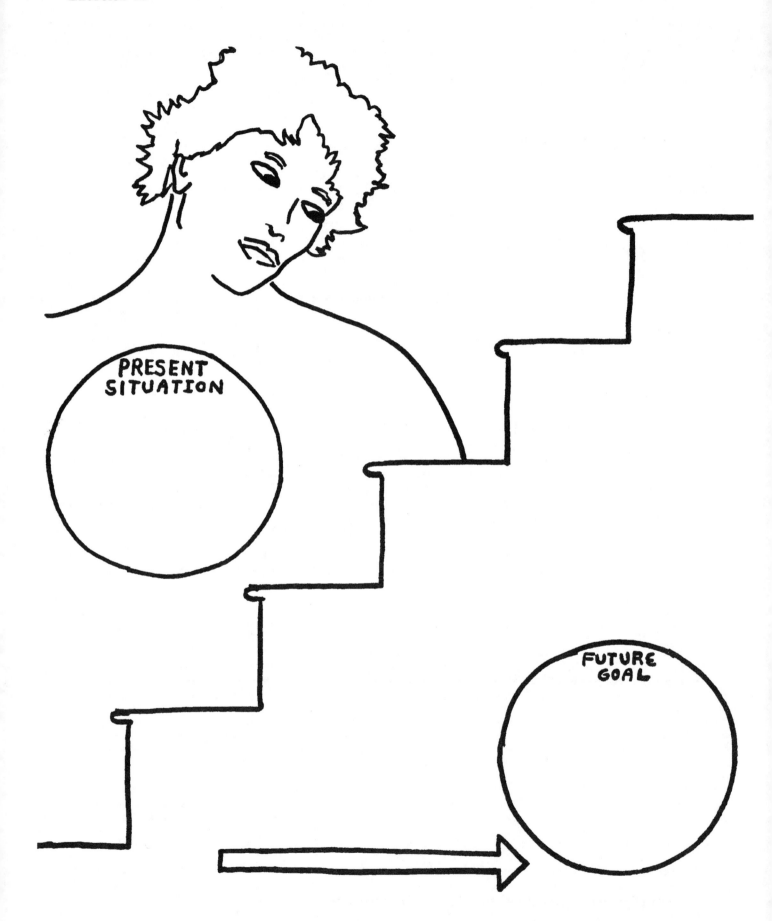

Exercise 16

PICTURE THIS

Purpose:

    1. To develop a climate for group interaction through self-disclosure.
    2. To recognize the impact of positive life experiences.

Materials:

    One photocopy of the illustration for each member; pencils, pens, markers, or crayons.

Description:

    A. The group leader asks members to describe the significance of photographs in people's lives.
    B. Each member is given the illustration of the blank photograph.
    C. Each member is asked to draw a memorable situation or experience from his or her life in the space provided.

Group Discussion:

    Members are encouraged to take turns discussing their drawings. They are asked to describe their feelings about the depicted scenes and how these and other memorable moments have had a significant impact on their lives. The group leader encourages members to ask questions and give feedback.

    During this discussion, the leader calls for both positive and negative experiences to be shared. This may be a way for members to gain insight into each other's personal history.

    This exercise is most useful in the early stages of group development when members are in the process of becoming acquainted with one another.

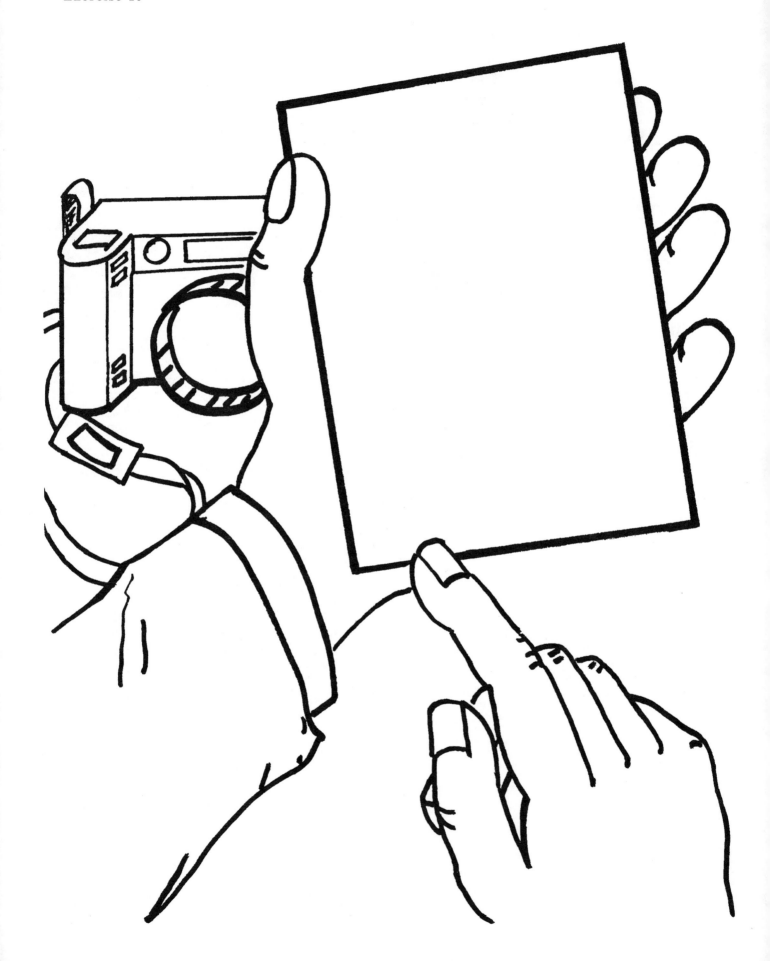

Exercise 17

WOULDN'T IT BE GREAT IF. . . ?

Purpose:

    1. To express individual needs through fantasy.
    2. To promote empathy.
    3. To enhance group cohesion through self-disclosure.

Materials:

    One photocopy of the illustration for each member; pencils, pens, markers, or crayons.

Description:

    A. The leader begins the discussion by introducing the idea that at one time or another, we have all thought to ourselves, "Wouldn't it be great if. . . ?" The leader relates this to the concept of a magician we could turn to magically change some aspect of our lives.
    B. As the materials are being distributed, members explore this concept.
    C. In the space below the magician's hat, members are asked to illustrate or describe something in their lives they have thought about changing. This could be something from either the past or the present.
    D. Group members are then told to imagine that a magician has granted their wish. They are asked to illustrate or describe that event in the space where something is seen coming out of the magician's hat.

Group Discussion:

    Members share their illustrations and are asked to describe that aspect of their life they wished could be changed, and the magical solution that has been granted. Common themes are focused on.

    Empathy is promoted by encouraging others to understand why each person would have preferred the changed event or experience.

    This exercise can be interpreted on many levels; therefore, it is effective with any group type at all stages of development.

Exercise 18

SOMEBODY FROM THE PAST

Purpose:

    1. To share the significance of other people in our lives.
    2. To develop insight through reminiscence.
    3. To promote group cohesion.

Materials:

    One photocopy of the illustration for each member; pencils, pens, markers, or crayons.

Description:

    A. The leader introduces the concept that certain people from the group members' past might add a great deal to a group session if they could somehow magically be made part of the group.
    B. The materials are distributed.
    C. On the pocketwatch, members are asked to illustrate the one person from their past they would most like to have participate in the group.

Group Discussion:

    Members share their illustration and describe the person from the past they chose to be part of the group. They relate the person's attributes and why he or she would add something special to the group.

    Members describe what they think people from the past would talk about, and their reactions to being part of the group. Members are asked to interpret what each other's choices reveal.

    Due to the open-ended nature of this exercise, it is effective with all group types, during all stages of development.

Exercise 18

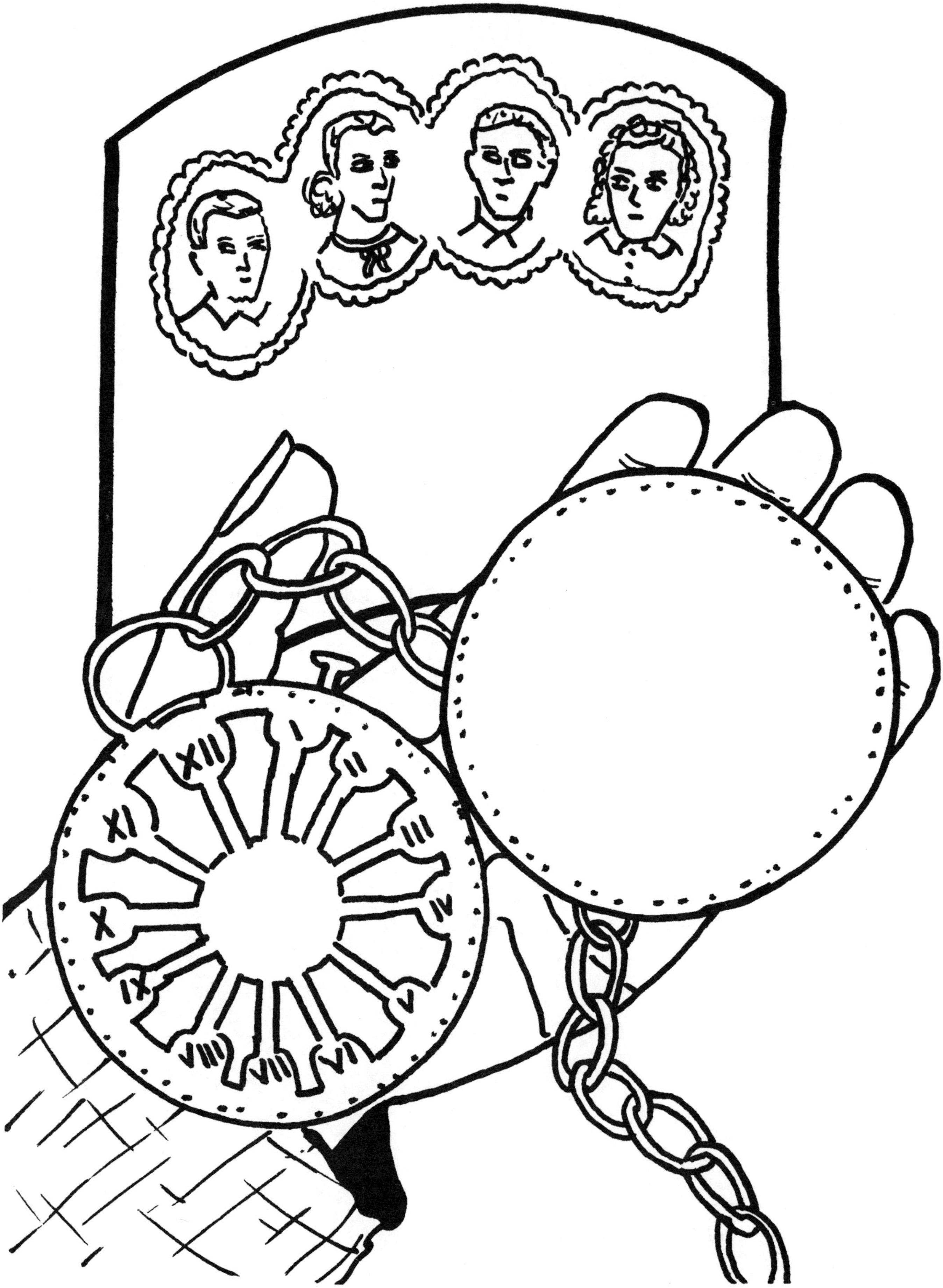

Exercise 19

ROUGH SEAS

Purpose:

    1. To explore ways of overcoming group conflicts and problems.
    2. To communicate concerns about the group experience.

Materials:

One photocopy of the illustration for each member; pencils, pens, markers, or crayons.

Description:

    A. The group leader engages members in a discussion of how every group has its share of obstacles and unexpected problems, just as a ship and its captain encounter when sailing alone on the high seas.
    B. Members are encouraged to explore some of the responsibilities they think a group leader should take to maintain purpose and direction within the group process.
    C. The materials are distributed.
    D. In the space provided on the captain's map, the members are asked to draw one or more of these difficult situations or experiences that may have already taken place within the group, or that they anticipate may lie ahead.

Group Discussion:

Members describe their illustrations. Similarities and differences in the way members view the group experience and the group leader are explored. The group leader calls for suggestions regarding the resolution of conflicts that may have been revealed.

This exercise can serve to give the group leader an understanding of what the group members need from the leader.

This exercise is effective with all group types in all stages of development as it may be interpreted on many levels.

Exercise 19

CAPTAIN'S MAP

FULL SPEED AHEAD

Purpose:

   1. To identify areas of resistance within the group.
   2. To promote group cohesion.
   3. To incorporate group feedback in problem solving.

Materials:

   One photocopy of the illustration for each member; pencils, pens, markers, or crayons.

Description:

   A. The group leader initiates the discussion by stating that from time to time all groups experience certain situations that may block their progress.
   B. As the materials are distributed, the leader relates the image of the train moving ahead on railroad tracks to the concept of the progress of the group. The roadblock on the track is equated with obstacles to group progress.
   C. On the picture of the roadblock, members are asked to illustrate a situation that has occurred during a group session which became an obstacle and prevented the group from moving along.

Group Discussion:

   Members share their illustrations and are encouraged to describe the obstacles they feel have obstructed the progress of the group. They may also be encouraged to communicate their feelings about these obstacles. Some of the ways these obstacles can be removed or changed to insure the continuing progress of the group are explored by the members.

   This exercise can be an effective method by which members may express conflict in an accepting and supportive environment. It requires an ability for insight and abstract reasoning. It is recommended for all stages of group development.

Exercise 21

THROWN FOR A LOOP

Purpose:

    1. To encourage empathy and insight.
    2. To reassure members that they can help one another.

Materials:

    One photocopy of the illustration for each member; pencils, pens, markers, or crayons.

Description:

    A. The leader initiates a discussion by suggesting that sometimes people are confronted with situations that at first seem to be very easy to deal with, but later prove to be troublesome.
    B. As the materials are being distributed, members comment on and explore the idea that at times they might be "thrown for a loop."
    C. In the space marked "At First . . .," members are asked to illustrate a situation or experience that at the outset seemed easy and uncomplicated.
    D. In the space marked "Then I Was Thrown For A Loop . . .," members illustrate how this situation or experience became more complicated.

Group Discussion:

    The leader asks group members to present their illustrations. The members are encouraged to describe the situation and relate the complication that "threw them for a loop." The leader asks whether or not they were able to deal successfully with this experience.
    Members comment and offer support.
    The leader helps group members to identify how this challenge may have led to feelings of anger, anxiety, conflict, or frustration.
    This exercise may be interpreted on many levels. Therefore it may be useful with groups in any stage of development, with any group type.

Exercise 22

THE SHOPPING MALL

Purpose:

1. To reveal oneself through fantasy.
2. To explore the needs of others through the expression of their wishes and desires.

Materials:

One photocopy of the illustration for each member; pencils, pens, markers, or crayons.

Description:

A. The leader engages the group in a discussion about how one's choice of objects and activities may reveal something about a person.
B. The leader introduces the idea that the type of merchandise someone might choose to sell, perhaps in a mall, may reveal something about that person as well.
C. While handing out the materials, the group leader goes on to describe an imaginary shopping mall, with empty stores.
D. The group members are asked to provide a name for one store and illustrate it with the type of objects or merchandise they would like to sell to the public.
E. In the remaining storefronts of this imaginary mall, members depict the names of the other stores and fill them with the items of merchandise they think fellow members might choose to sell.

Group Discussion:

Members share their illustrations. They describe their own stores and the significance of what they chose to sell. Group members are encouraged to help each other recognize what their choices reveal about themselves. The group explores how these choices might relate to immediate needs or special memories.

Members also describe what they illustrated for fellow members. The reasons for these choices are explored.

This exercise is nonthreatening and can be interpreted on many levels. Therefore it is effective with a variety of groups, at all stages of development.

STAR
★
MALL

SALE
TODAY!

ERASE THAT!

Purpose:

    1. To promote a better understanding of group dynamics.
    2. To explore common needs in order to promote group cohesion.

Materials:

One photocopy of the illustration for each member; pencils, pens, markers, or crayons.

Description:

    A. The group leader begins by telling members that they will be talking about their experiences within the group. The leader focuses the discussion on each member's role, and how individual behavior can add or detract from the quality of the group.
    B. Members are assured that they can develop constructive alternatives to problems within the group.
    C. Materials are distributed. Members are asked to relate the theme being discussed to the illustration.
    D. In the space provided, members are asked to illustrate a problem they feel impedes or interferes with the flow of their group.

Group Discussion:

The group leader asks the members to describe their illustrated problem to the rest of the group. They are encouraged to find constructive ways to solve the problems discussed, and offer support to each other.

Common themes are focused on.

This exercise may help group members to better understand how groups function. It may motivate members to work toward goals and find positive ways to further the group process.

This exercise may be useful for groups in the middle to later stages of group development, with members capable of abstract reasoning.

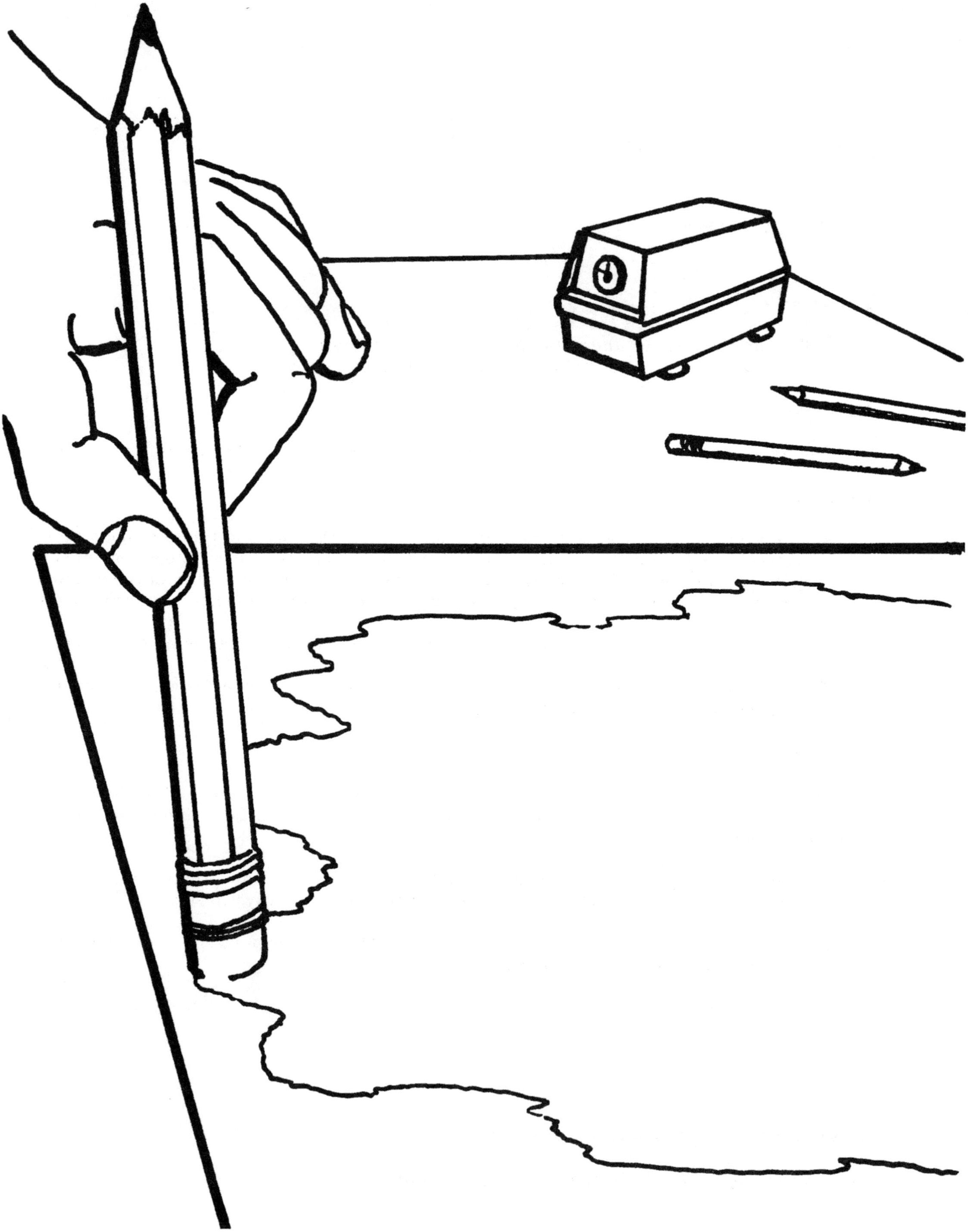

Exercise 24

CUTTING THE APRON STRINGS

Purpose:

    1. To identify the significance of other people in our lives.
    2. To promote personal insight through self-disclosure.

Materials:

One photocopy of the illustration for each member; pencils, pens, markers, or crayons.

Description:

    A. The leader introduces the idea that certain people have a great deal of influence over us. At times, it might seem difficult to let go of these people.
    B. As the materials are distributed, members are asked to comment on how the illustration relates to the discussion.
    C. In the space provided, members draw someone who has had great influence over their lives. This can be someone they may or may not have been able to let go of.
    D. On the attached apron strings, members write a description of one type of influence someone has had over them.
    E. On the cut apron strings, members write a description of how they may have managed to free themselves from the same influence or another person's influence.

Group Discussion:

Members share their illustration and describe in detail how they were influenced by the depicted person. The member describes the attributes of the person depicted. Whether this was a good or bad influence over their life is explored.

This exercise is effective with groups whose members are capable of abstract thinking, in any stage of development.

Exercise 25

WHEN I WAS A CHILD

Purpose:

    1. To share fantasies in order to promote heightened awareness of self and others.
    2. Exploration of role models.
    3. Identification of interpersonal needs.

Materials:

One photocopy of the illustration for each member; pencils, pens, markers, or crayons.

Description:

    A. The group leader initiates a discussion about how all children like to imagine being a grownup. Members are asked to reminisce about themselves as children, and what they thought they would like to be as adults.
    B. As the materials are distributed, the leader helps members to explore ways the illustration relates to this theme.
    C. Group members are asked to illustrate how, as children, they fantasized themselves as adults.

Group Discussion:

Members describe their illustrations. They are asked to discuss possible role models from their childhood, and how they may have been influenced by them as they grew up. Similarities and differences between the members are compared. In some instances, members will reveal disappointments.

Members are encouraged to be supportive of one another and ask questions about the experiences and relationships revealed.

This exercise may be interpreted on many levels. It may be useful with a variety of groups whose members are well acquainted with each other.

Exercise 26

PUTTING IT ON THE BACK BURNER

Purpose:

    1. To provide an atmosphere for group cohesion.
    2. To express conflict in a supportive environment.
    3. To understand group dynamics.

Materials:

One photocopy of the illustration for each group member; pencils, pens, markers, or crayons.

Description:

    A. The leader asks the group members to discuss the meaning of the expression "putting it on the back burner."
    B. The leader introduces the concept that there are many issues that the group discusses that do not get resolved or addressed right away, and therefore are "put on the back burner."
    C. As the materials are distributed, the leader asks the members to think of an issue or situation that may have occurred during a group session that they feel merits further discussion.
    D. In the space provided on each burner, members are asked to write or illustrate such an issue or situation.

Group Discussion:

Members share their illustrations and describe what they have depicted. Members focus on the situation and issues revealed. Any similarities or differences are highlighted by the group leader.

Members are invited to explore some of the possible reasons that these issues were not able to be resolved at the time they occurred.

Members are encouraged to offer suggestions on how to deal with these issues in the future.

This exercise is effective with groups who are capable of abstract reasoning, in the middle to later stages of group development.

Exercise 27

STIRRING UP TROUBLE

Purpose:

1. To understand the consequences of behavior.
2. To explore responses to peer pressure.
3. To enhance group identity and cohesion.

Materials:

One photocopy of the illustration for each member; pencils, pens, markers, or crayons.

Description:

A. The group leader introduces the idea that our behavior can sometimes be influenced by others, not always in a positive way.
B. As the materials are handed out, the group leader initiates a discussion about the meaning of peer pressure.
C. The group leader asks the members to relate the illustration to the theme of "stirring up trouble."
D. In the space provided, members are asked to draw a situation or experience they have participated in, which may have been influenced by someone else, resulting in a negative outcome.

Group Discussion:

Group members are encouraged to reveal themselves by describing their drawing. The group leader helps the members explore the influences that led them to take action. The leader encourages members to question and comment about related events and feelings.

Often, this exercise evolves into a discussion of how others may exert power over us. Members are asked to offer reassurance and suggestions about dealing with these types of situations in the future.

This exercise encourages members to reveal many types of negative experiences and situations in a supportive environment. It is effective with groups that have established some degree of trust between members and are in the middle to later stages of group development.

Exercise 28

IRONING OUT THE WRINKLES

Purpose:

    1. To recognize individual concerns about the group process.
    2. To reinforce the role of group decision making.
    3. To promote group identity and cohesion.

Materials:

    One photocopy of the illustration for each member; pencils, pens, markers, or crayons.

Description:

    A. The group leader encourages members to explore the meaning of the phrase "ironing out the wrinkles." The leader relates the illustration to suggestions about improving the group process.
    B. The materials are distributed. Group members are told to illustrate on the wrinkled cloth a problem within the group process that they feel needs to be "ironed out."
    C. Members are asked to illustrate on the iron one constructive suggestion about how to improve this perceived problem.

Discussion:

    Each member describes the problem he or she thinks is creating a "wrinkle" in the group process. The leader encourages other members to offer feedback and comments about the described problem. Then the member is invited to offer a proposed solution which could "iron out" the problem.

    Suggestions which are similar are focused on. Members are asked to share ideas on the ways some of these proposed changes might be accomplished.

    Because this exercise affords members an opportunity to evaluate some of the negative aspects of the group process, it is practical with any group type at all stages of development.

    At a later date, it may be useful to review the original responses to this exercise, to assess whether any of the proposed solutions have been successfully implemented.

Exercise 29

THE FAMILY TREE

Purpose:

    1. To describe the significance of other people in our lives.
    2. To increase understanding and acceptance of others.

Materials:

One photocopy of the illustration for each member; pencils, pens, markers, or crayons.

Description:

    A. The group leader begins by describing this exercise as a way for members to share details about the significant people in their lives.
    B. The group leader introduces the concept of a "family tree" as a way of showing how people are connected to each other. For the purposes of this exercise, the family tree may also include significant people who may or may not be related directly to the member.
    C. The materials are distributed. In the apples on the tree, the members are asked to draw the people who have played an important part in their lives.
    D. In the apples at the bottom of the illustration, members may illustrate some of the people in their lives who are missed because they are no longer part of their "family tree."

Group Discussion:

Members describe each person they have illustrated on their family tree and share the experiences they have had with these people. These may be positive or negative.

The leader invites other members to ask questions and explore the significance of the role these people have played in the member's life. When a member relates negative experiences, other members are encouraged to be supportive and reassuring.

Because of the self-revelation involved in this exercise, this exercise is most effective with groups well acquainted with each other, in the middle to later stages of group development.

Exercise 30

PUSHING THE BUTTONS

Purpose:

    1. To provide an opportunity for expressing anger and frustration.
    2. To enhance group identity and cohesion.

Materials:

    One photocopy of the illustration for each group member; pencils, pens, markers, or crayons.

Description:

    A. The group leader begins the exercise by describing the group's interpersonal relationships as very complex. They are both negative and positive. The group leader goes on to explain that there are times during the group process when some of the members may feel anger and frustration.
    B. As the materials are distributed, the meaning of the expression "pushing one's buttons" is examined.
    C. Members discuss the way the illustration relates to this theme, and how it pertains to times during the group when individual members may experience anger or frustration.
    D. In the space provided, members are asked to draw or write a situation, feeling, or event that has occurred during the group that "pushed their buttons" and made them feel angry or frustrated.

Discussion:

    Members share their illustrations and describe what happened to "push their buttons." The leader encourages the members to discuss the significance of these events or experiences. This can be an opportunity to explore how the group process was affected at the time they happened.
    The rest of the group is invited to comment and offer suggestions about how to cope with these types of events.
    This exercise is often effective with groups in the middle to later stages of development.

Exercise 31

THE JIGSAW PUZZLE

Purpose:

    1. To evaluate one's role in the group process.
    2. To promote group identity and cohesion.
    3. To promote an understanding of group dynamics.

Materials:

    One photocopy of the illustration for each member; pencils, pens, markers, or crayons.

Description:

    A. The group leader introduces the idea that every member of the group, including the leader, has a role in contributing to the character, substance, and quality of the group. The leader explains that these roles are interconnected, like the pieces of a jigsaw puzzle.
    B. The materials are distributed, and the way this theme relates to the illustration of a puzzle with interconnected pieces is explored.
    C. In the space provided, group members are asked to illustrate their individual roles as they themselves see them. Optionally, they may also choose to illustrate the leader's role as they see it.

Group Discussion:

    Members describe their pieces of the puzzle and the way they view both their own role and the leader's role. As they describe each piece of the puzzle, the group leader attaches the sheets together to form a large puzzle.

    The group leader encourages members to share comments, offer support, and make suggestions about improving the group process.

    This exercise is effective with groups well acquainted with each other, in the middle to later stages of group development.

MEMBER

GROUP LEADER

TOP SECRET!

Purpose:

1. To facilitate an atmosphere for self-disclosure.
2. To recognize the needs of others.
3. To understand the importance of confidentiality.

Materials:

One photocopy of the illustration for each member; pencils, pens, markers, or crayons.

Description:

A. The group leader introduces the idea that we all have feelings about certain experiences that we try to keep private and secret.
B. The materials are given out, and the theme is related to the picture of the child playing detective.
C. Group members are asked to draw something that he or she feels is private but is nevertheless willing to share with the group.

Group Discussion:

Each member presents his or her illustration. The leader encourages the member to explore the significance of the drawing. The feelings that the member has about sharing this with the group is also explored.

Group members are invited to ask questions about the experiences or relationships depicted.

The idea of sharing secret feelings with group members is examined.

This exercise often evolves into a discussion of the importance of confidentiality as part of the group process. Because of the open-ended nature of this exercise, it is effective with all group types in the middle to later stages of development.

Exercise 33

THE WORLD ON MY SHOULDERS

Purpose:

    1. To identify and clarify feelings about stressful situations.
    2. To facilitate group interaction by sharing personal information.
    3. To develop empathy in order to understand the needs of others.

Materials:

One photocopy of the illustration for each member; pencils, pens, markers, or crayons.

Description:

    A. The group leader begins the exercise by encouraging members to define the meaning of stress, and how this relates to the phrase "the world on my shoulders."
    B. Materials are distributed, and the leader encourages free association about the illustration and the theme.
    C. In the space provided, members illustrate a situation or experience that provokes stress.

Group Discussion:

Members describe their illustration to the group. They are encouraged to reveal how the experiences or situations they have depicted make them feel burdened by stress.

The rest of the group is invited to offer their interpretations, as well as possible suggestions about how to manage these situations.

Members may develop mutual understanding and acceptance as they share similar experiences.

This exercise is useful in the middle to later stages of group development.

Exercise 34

TO THE RESCUE!

Purpose:

    1. To promote a better understanding about group dynamics.
    2. To develop insight about one's role in the group process.

Materials:

One photocopy of the illustration for each member; pencils, pens, markers, or crayons.

Description:

    A. The group leader introduces the idea that all groups sometimes experience difficult, troublesome situations, and that certain members take an active part in helping to solve problems.
    B. The illustration is distributed and related to the theme. The group leader explains that the splashing water is the difficult group situation. The person in the picture is the rescuer. The life preserver is the method of helping.
    C. In the splashing water, members are asked to draw the real or imagined situation that challenges the group as a whole. On the body of the rescuer they are also asked to identify those members they think most often take the role of rescuer when the group encounters difficult situations. On the life preserver, they are asked to describe the method of helping.

Group Discussion:

Members share their drawings. After describing the troublesome situation and the method of helping, they are asked to convey the personal traits of the member they have chosen as rescuer. Other members are encouraged to explore these choices through comments and questions.

By comparing the positive and negative aspects observed by the group members, members may be encouraged to find constructive ways to further develop the group process.

A variety of groups at all stages of development should find this exercise effective.

Exercise 35

A SERIOUS MATTER

Purpose:

1. To identify issues and feelings of concern.
2. To enhance group identity and cohesion.

Materials:

One photocopy of the illustration for each member; pencils, pens, markers, or crayons.

Description:

A. The leader describes the exercise as one in which members will be relying on either their memories or their imagination.
B. They are asked to imagine a serious conversation between an adult and a child.
C. The materials are distributed.
D. Members are asked to write or illustrate in the space provided at the top of the picture what they think the depicted man and child might be talking about.

Group Discussion:

Members describe the conversation. They are asked to comment on the significance of what has been remembered or imagined, and to describe the relationship this conversation could have to their own lives.

They explore not only what is being said, but what they think the feelings of the depicted figures are.

Members are encouraged to reveal whether this conversation actually took place.

Because of the self-revelation inherent in this exercise, it is effective with well-integrated groups whose members are able to think abstractly.

Exercise 36

TUG OF WAR

Purpose:

    1. To develop insight about self-image.
    2. To promote understanding of opposing emotions.

Materials:

One photocopy of the illustration; pencils, pens, markers, or crayons.

Description:

    A. The group leader explains to the group members that people often are in conflict because of opposing feelings.
    B. The group members are given the illustration.
    C. The group leader asks for initial reactions to the phrase "tug of war." This theme is then expanded so that members can describe how this might apply to struggles within oneself.
    D. The members are asked to draw or write one type of feeling in one box of the illustration. He or she is then asked to draw or write a conflicting feeling in the other box.

Group Discussion:

Members are asked to describe what has been drawn or written on the illustration. The leader initiates a discussion about how these conflicting emotions can affect the members' self-image.

This exercise may help group members define the significant components that underlie conflicting feelings. Group members are encouraged to share feelings about the need to integrate and resolve these opposing feelings.

This exercise is useful in the middle to later stages of group development. It is most appropriate with clients who are well acquainted with each other, so they are not threatened by the level of self-disclosure.

Exercise 36

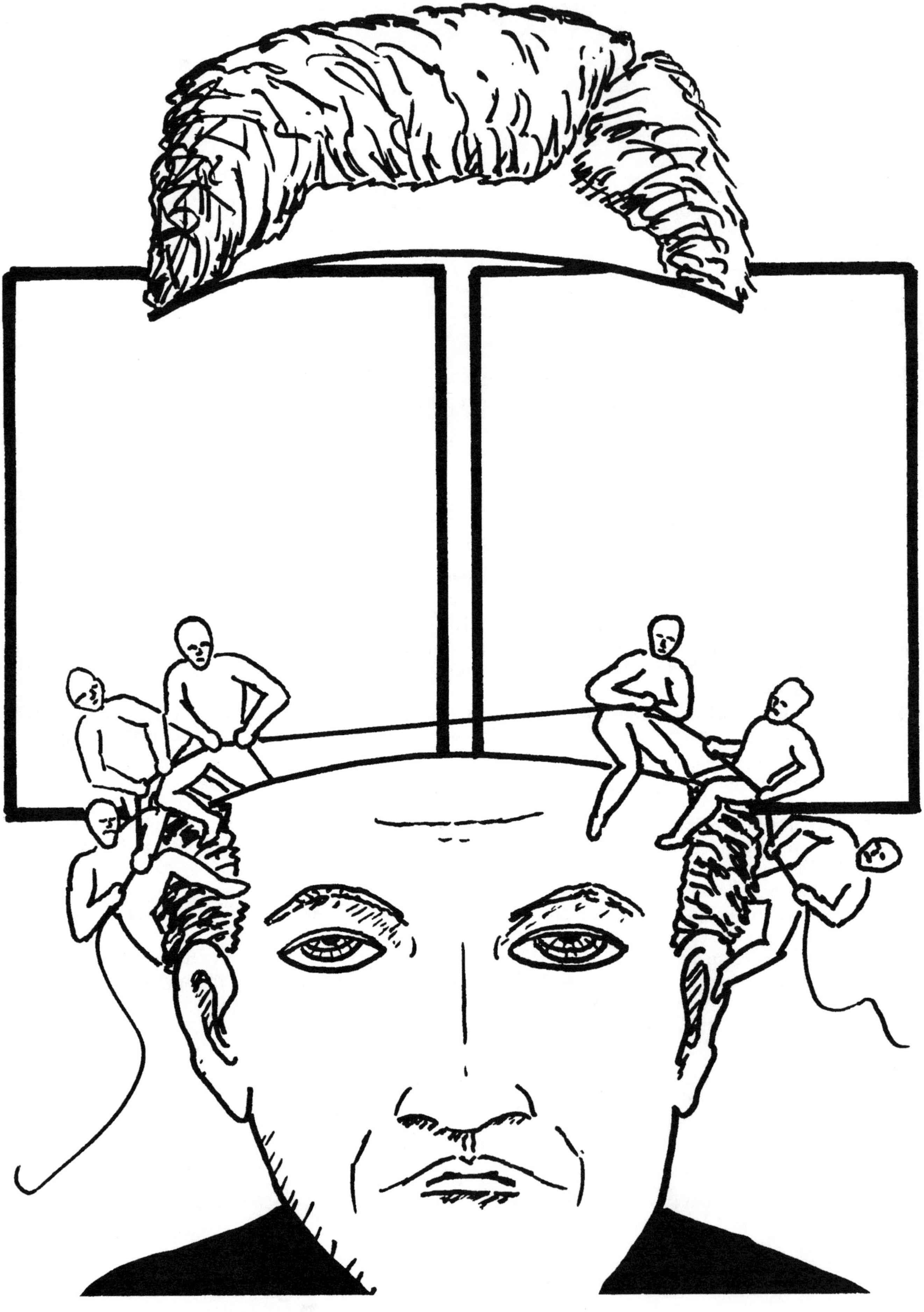

Exercise 37

LETTING THE CAT OUT OF THE BAG

Purpose:

    1. To elicit group input when formulating group goals.
    2. To identify significant issues in the group process.

Materials:

One photocopy of the illustration for each member; pencils, pens, markers, or crayons.

Description:

    A. The group leader explains that it is common for group members to have mixed feelings about discussing sensitive issues and emotions which come up during group sessions.
    B. The materials are distributed. The group members are asked to explore how this theme might relate to the saying "letting the cat out of the bag."
    C. In the space provided, the group members are encouraged to illustrate a sensitive situation, experience, or feeling that has been uncovered during group sessions which should be examined further, however reluctant they may be to do so.

Group Discussion:

The group members are asked to describe their drawings. The group leader invites them to focus on the issue, feeling, or experience that has come up. Other members are asked to comment and offer support.

Together, the group leader and members may try to suggest ways to further explore these themes and integrate them into the future course of the group.

This exercise may be useful in the middle to later stages of group development, with members who are capable of abstract reasoning.

Exercise 38

JUDGE AND JURY

Purpose:

1. To promote problem solving.
2. To understand the dynamics of group decision making.

Materials:

One photocopy of the illustration for each member; pencils, pens, markers, or crayons.

Description:

A. The group leader asks members to think about a recurring negative situation that takes place either in their group or the setting in which they reside, which causes conflict or controversy.
B. While handing out the materials, members are asked to imagine they are part of a courtroom scene, where the situation will be presented to a jury and, hopefully, a solution will be found.
C. In the space provided, members write or illustrate the negative situation.

Group Discussion:

Each participant describes his or her negative situation. The leader encourages others to act as members of a jury and ask questions about the described situation.

Other members may take turns acting as the judge and attempt to guide the discussion.

The leader helps members explore feelings and common themes. The members are invited to seek ways to find a solution or overcome the difficulties described.

Because of the open-ended format of this exercise, it may be effective with all group types during all stages of group development.

Exercise 39

BLOWING YOUR TOP

Purpose:

1. To provide an opportunity to express feelings of anger.
2. To identify appropriate means of dealing with anger.
3. To reinforce trust through self-disclosure.

Materials:

One photocopy of the illustration for each member; pencils, pens, markers, or crayons.

Description:

A. The leader begins the exercise by introducing the idea that at times situations occur during group sessions as well as members' own lives that can make them feel angry.
B. The various ways people choose to deal with, avoid, or channel their anger becomes a focus for discussion.
C. The materials are distributed. The illustration of someone "blowing their top" is related to the discussion.
D. In the space provided, members are asked to write or draw a situation that has developed within the group or their own lives that makes them feel very angry.
E. On the back of the photocopy, members list several possible ways to deal with this anger.

Group Discussion:

First, each member shares with the group what has made them angry. Then, other members are encouraged to suggest ways to deal with the situation. This is compared with what the member wrote on the reverse of the photocopy.

This exercise is appropriate for groups who are well acquainted with each other, in the later stages of group development.

Exercise 40

THE MIND READER

Purpose:

1. To identify and interpret individual needs.
2. To build trust.

Materials:

One photocopy of the illustration for each member; pencils, pens, markers, or crayons.

Description:

A. The group leader introduces the idea that there are times during the group when something is bothering an individual, and he or she is not able to talk about it. Further, that individual might wish that either the leader or other members of the group were "mind readers," so that they would be able to readily comprehend what was troubling that individual and offer support.
B. The illustration is distributed and related to the theme of wishing that others in the group were mind readers.
C. In the space provided, the leader asks members to illustrate an issue, experience, or problem the member would like to be focused on at this time in the group experience.

Group Discussion:

Members describe their illustration. The significance of what has been depicted is discussed. The group explores the issues presented, through comments and questions.

The leader helps the group to identify feelings and common themes, and encourages members to be supportive of each other. The members help the individual focus on ways the issues can be dealt with during the course of future groups.

Because of the self-revelation involved, this exercise is effective with groups whose members are capable of abstract reasoning, in the middle to later stages of group development.

Exercise 41

THE TIGHTROPE

Purpose:

1. To provide an atmosphere for group cohesion.
2. To understand group dynamics.
3. To encourage members to demonstrate empathy and support.

Materials:

One photocopy of the illustration for each member; pencils, pens, markers, or crayons.

Description:

A. The leader introduces the idea that the group is able to offer support whenever members encounter difficult problems and challenges. Some examples might be the death of a family member, loss of a job, medical problems, and so on.
B. The metaphor of the group holding a net while the member holds a tightrope is related to this discussion.
C. The materials are distributed. Members are asked to write or draw on the tightrope walker's flag a description of a problem or challenge that occurred to themselves or another member of the group.
D. On the space provided on the safety net at the bottom of the illustration, members are asked to write or draw an illustration of how the group demonstrated its support.

Group Discussion:

The group members are asked to share their illustrations and describe in detail both the problem and the way the group offered support. They are encouraged to explore the feelings surrounding the episode and the group's subsequent support. Common themes are focused on.

When memories about past conflict or discord within the group surface, members may offer suggestions on ways they can be of greater support to one another in the future.

This exercise is effective with all group types, in the middle to later stages of development.

Exercise 41

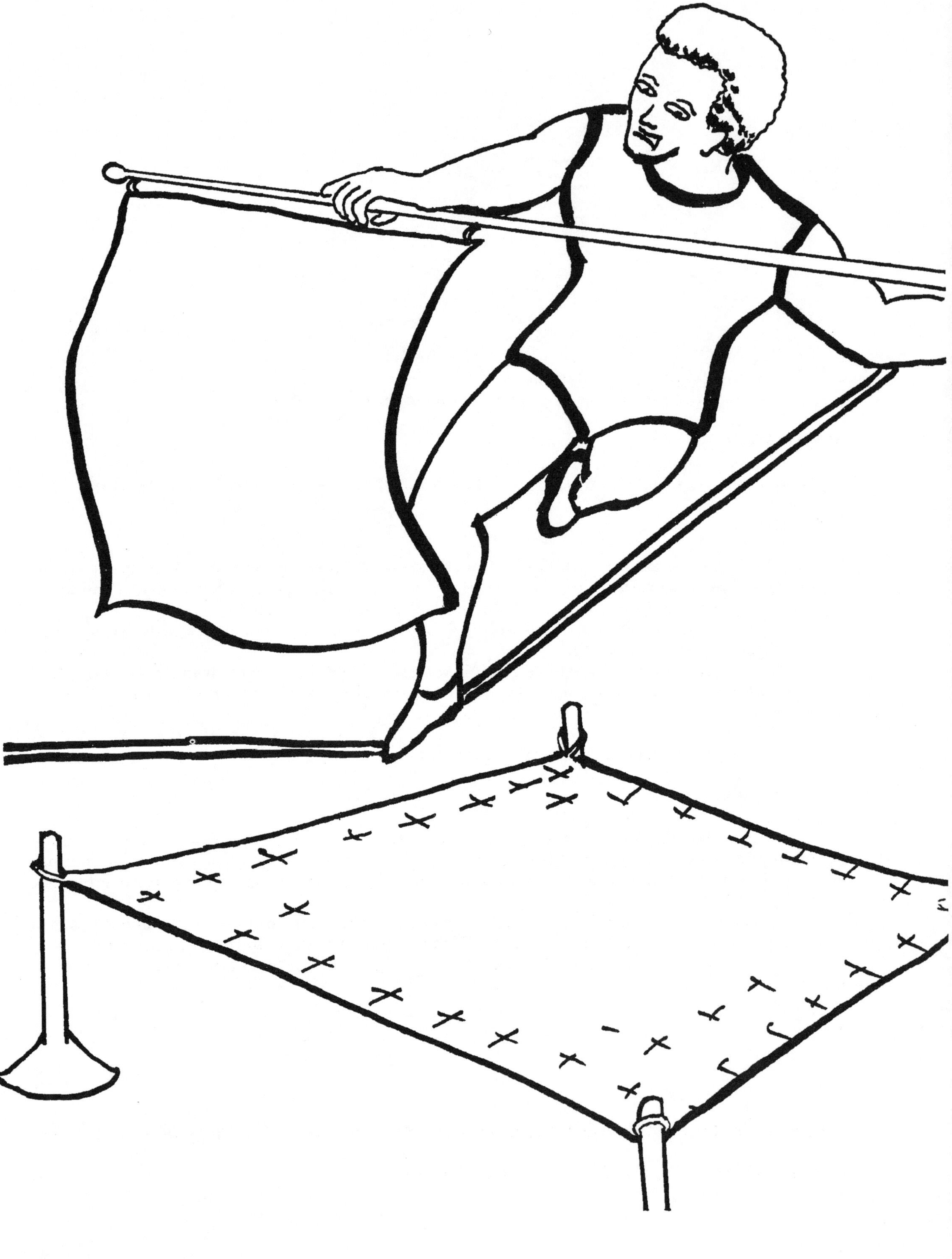

Exercise 42

TAKING A ROLE

Purpose:

1. To evaluate one's role in the group.
2. To promote group identity and cohesion.
3. To understand group dynamics.

Materials:

One photocopy of the illustration for each member; pencils, pens, markers, or crayons.

Description:

A. The group leader introduces the idea that every individual in the group has a role and plays an important part in the functioning of the group.
B. Members are encouraged to describe how individual roles add to the unique identity of the group.
C. The materials are distributed. Members are asked to illustrate themselves on the silhouette and think about what role they may play in the group process.

Group Discussion:

The group leader encourages members to describe their roles within the group. Other members are asked to comment.

The group leader helps the members to focus on how each member adds to the group identity.

Group members often add constructively to the discussion, commenting on the personal strengths and qualities of each member.

This exercise is effective with any group type in all stages of group development. By offering peer support, this exercise may help the guarded member to be more open.

Exercise 42

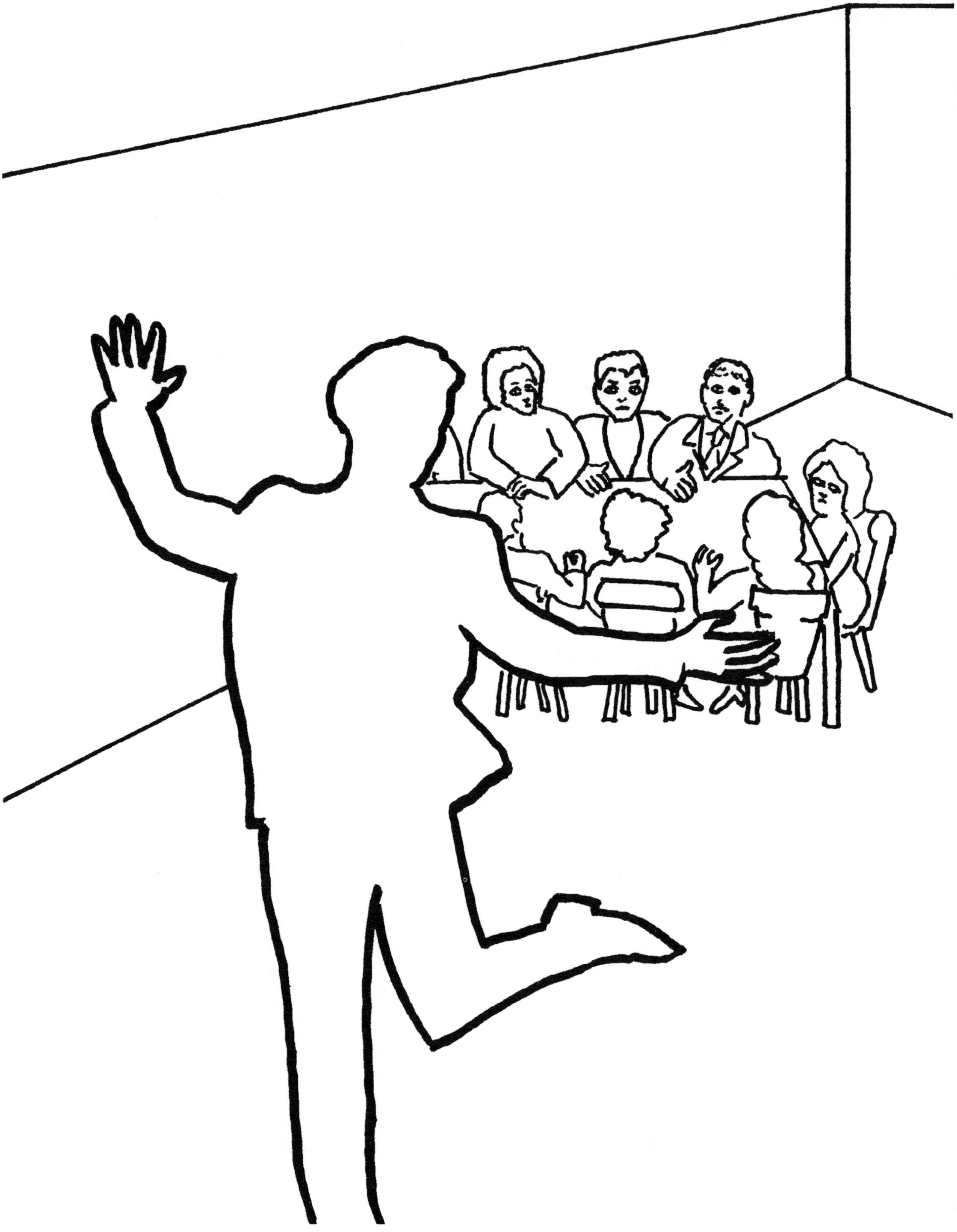

Exercise 43

IN YOUR SHELL

Purpose:

    1. To incorporate group feedback into self-evaluation.
    2. To promote empathy and understanding.
    3. To build trust within the group.

Materials:

    One photocopy of the illustration for each member; pencils, pens, markers, or crayons.

Description:

    A. The group leader introduces the idea that during the course of the group there are times when a member may feel like backing away.
    B. The group members are encouraged to identify some of the reasons this might happen.
    C. The materials are distributed. In panel number one of the illustration located at the top of the page, members are told to draw an experience or feeling which in the past may have precipitated the need to back away and withdraw into a "shell," as illustrated in panel number two.
    D. In panel number three, the member is asked to illustrate or write some of the reasons for being able to come out of the shell.

Group Discussion:

    Members share their illustrations. The leader helps the members to examine the feelings that prompted them to withdraw (and, if appropriate, to emerge once again). Situations will differ, but common themes will emerge and should be focused on.

    Through this exercise, troubling emotions, feelings, or situations may be revealed. The group should be encouraged to follow through on other ways they can continue to help each other resolve difficulties.

    The exercise is effective during middle to later stages of development with groups that are well acquainted with one another.

Exercise 44

THE BAGGAGE I CARRY

Purpose:

    1. To identify unresolved group issues.
    2. To create a supportive group environment.

Materials:

One photocopy of the illustration for each member; pencils, pens, markers, or crayons.

Description:

    A. The group leader introduces the metaphor that past problems of the group that remain unresolved are burdens, much like heavy baggage that has to be carried around.
    B. The materials are distributed, and the way the theme relates to the illustration is explored with the members.
    C. On each piece of luggage, the members are asked to illustrate an unresolved issue that has come up during past group sessions which they think should be addressed further.

Group Discussion:

Group members share their illustrations. Each member describes in detail the unresolved issue they have illustrated. The group leader encourages comments and discussion of the issues presented. Suggestions by members for enhancing the group process are explored.

This exercise may be a useful tool in helping the leader to assess each individual member's group experience and group satisfaction. It is effective with groups in the middle to later stages of development.

Exercise 45

THE UMBRELLA

Purpose:

    1. To understand the importance of defense mechanisms.
    2. To explore difficult situations in a nonthreatening way.

Materials:

One photocopy of the illustration for each member; pencils, pens, markers, or crayons.

Description:

    A. The group leader introduces the idea that everyone is vulnerable to feeling hurt at one time or another. The group leader explores some of the ways that people protect themselves from upsetting situations or feelings.
    B. The materials are distributed. The concept of an umbrella as protection against the rain is examined, as well as how it feels to be under a rain cloud without an umbrella.
    C. In the space provided inside the picture of the rain cloud, the members are asked to draw an experience or situation which could be difficult or upsetting. On the umbrella itself, the members are asked to draw one way of defending themselves against the situation or experience they drew in the rain cloud.

Group Discussion:

Group members are asked to describe the situation or experience illustrated. They are asked to examine the feelings associated with this situation or experience, as well as the way the difficult situation or experience was dealt with at the time.

Group members are encouraged to explore ways they think they might help one another if difficulties were to arise in the future.

This exercise may be useful with groups in the middle to later stages of development, whose members are able to think abstractly.

Exercise 46

I REACT

Purpose:

1. To identify stressful situations.
2. To compare different coping techniques.

Materials:

One photocopy of the illustration for each member; pencils, pens, markers, or crayons.

Description:

A. The leader begins the exercise by introducing the subject of stress. Members share feelings about the meaning of the word and how it affects their lives.
B. As the materials are distributed, the leader uses the illustration to introduce the concept of how people deal with stress in a variety of ways.
C. Four boxes appear on the illustration. In the first three boxes, members are asked to write or draw some stressful situations they might respond to in the manner depicted.
D. In the fourth box, they are asked to reverse the task, and illustrate a way they have chosen to deal with stress in the past.

Group Discussion:

Members share their examples of stressful situations, and are asked to describe how these situations made them feel. In addition, the leader encourages members to examine the reasons they chose their particular method of lessening stress. Fellow members comment on their choices. Alternate ways to reduce stress are explored.

This exercise is useful with groups in the middle to later stages of development, with members who are capable of abstract reasoning.

I REACT

LIKE SO

THIS WAY

LIKE THIS

ANOTHER WAY

Exercise 48

THE GRAB BAG

Purpose:

1. To identify different viewpoints and perspectives.
2. To increase understanding of group dynamics.

Materials:

One photocopy of the illustration for each member; pencils, pens, markers, or crayons.

Description:

A. The leader introduces the idea that when first entering a group, members may have preconceived ideas of what their group experience will be like and what they will gain from it.
B. As the materials are distributed, the common experience of being surprised by some of the unexpected things that have developed during group participation is explored. This idea is compared to the concept of finding something unexpected in a "grab bag."
C. In the space provided, the members are asked to illustrate something both positive and unexpected that was derived from his or her group experience.

Group Discussion:

Members share their illustrations and are asked to describe the positive and unexpected developments that occurred during their participation in the group.

The leader asks them to contrast this with their initial expectations when they first began participating in the group.

The leader helps members explore feelings about some of the unfulfilled expectations they may still have.

This exercise may be effective with groups in the middle to later stages of development, with any group type. It is interesting to examine why some members share rewarding feelings about the group and others do not.

Exercise 49

BURYING YOUR HEAD IN THE SAND

Purpose:

1. To identify feelings of discomfort.
2. To develop new coping styles.
3. To give empathy and reassurance.

Materials:

One photocopy of the illustration for each member; pencils, pens, markers, or crayons.

Description:

A. While handing out the materials, the group leader asks members to think about the idea that wanting to bury and forget unpleasant experiences is a universal feeling.
B. The group leader asks the group members to describe how this theme relates to the illustration of the ostrich burying his head in the sand.
C. In the depicted underground space, the client is asked to illustrate an uncomfortable situation or experience he or she may have buried and does not want to think or talk about.

Group Discussion:

The group leader invites members to describe their illustrations to the rest of the group. Group members are encouraged to be supportive and ask questions about the situation or experience revealed. Members are asked to offer constructive suggestions on how to deal with these situations.

Members focus on the possible consequences of forever burying these unpleasant experiences.

This exercise encourages members to reveal many types of negative situations and experiences in a supportive environment. It is most effective with groups that have established some degree of trust between members, and are in the later stages of group development.

Exercise 50

SHELTER FROM THE STORM

Purpose:

    1. To identify concerns within the group.
    2. To increase group cohesion.

Materials:

    One photocopy of the illustration for each group member; pencils, pens, markers, or crayons.

Description:

    A. The group leader introduces the concept of finding "shelter from the storm." Members discuss this and relate it to the need to feel safe and secure in their group.
    B. As the materials are distributed, members explore this theme as it relates to the depicted shelter from a storm.
    C. On the storm clouds, members are asked to illustrate a problem or issue they have confronted in the past or are currently dealing with; they may also illustrate in the shelter itself how the group has provided some help with this issue.
    D. If appropriate, members may choose to illustrate issues or problems that the group has not been able to help them with.

Group Discussion:

    Members are asked to share their illustrations and present the positive ways that being in the group has helped them with the problem or issue they have described. Unresolved issues are presented as well. The leader encourages constructive suggestions from other members on how to best deal with these issues in the future.

    This exercise may help members identify individual problem areas, as well as provide members with an opportunity to offer suggestions for improving the overall functioning of the group.

    As this exercise may be interpreted on many levels, it may be useful in the middle to later stages of group development, with any group type.

Exercise 51

NO ONE CAN FILL THOSE SHOES

Purpose:

1. To explore feelings about terminations.
2. To understand group dynamics
3. To promote group cohesion.

Materials:

One photocopy of the illustration for each group member; pencils, pens, markers, or crayons.

Description:

A. The group leader introduces the theme that each member plays an important role in the group.
B. Members are encouraged to explore how the group process is affected when someone leaves the group.
C. The materials are distributed.
D. In the circular spaces provided, members are told to illustrate some of the qualities of the individual who is terminating that have made this individual special, unique, and important to the group process.

Discussion:

Members share their illustrations. They are asked to describe the special qualities of the individual who is leaving the group. The leader asks for reasons they will be missed. The member being described is given an opportunity to tell whether he or she agrees with these observations.

This exercise gives group members an opportunity to express positive feelings about a terminating member, as well as serve to identify how this loss may impact on the group's dynamics.

This exercise may also be useful in the event of a group leader terminating.

This exercise is recommended for groups in all stages of development, with all group types.

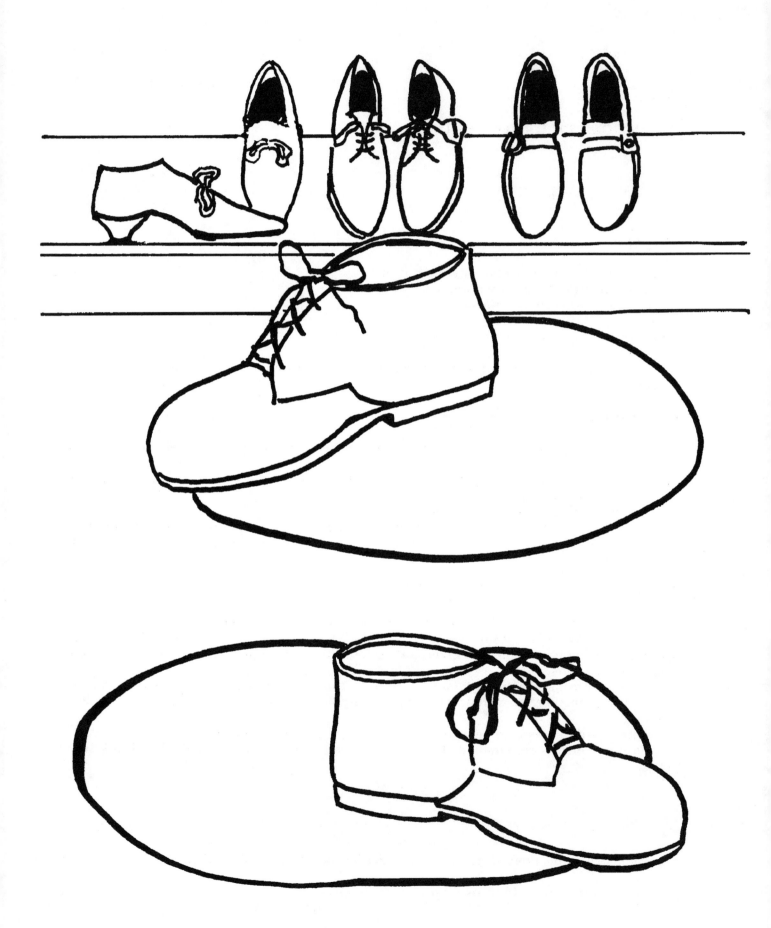

Exercise 52

THE NEW KEYS

Purpose:

1. To incorporate group feedback into self-evaluation.
2. To encourage interpersonal bonding and group cohesion.

Materials:

One photocopy of the illustration for each member; pencils, pens, markers, or crayons.

Description:

A. The group leader introduces the idea that during the course of group sessions, coping strategies may be developed by the members to help them deal with different situations.
B. The group leader and the members explore this, relating the idea of coping skills to the concept of an imaginary key holder with keys that help unlock doors to understanding.
C. The materials are distributed.
D. On each key holder in the illustration, members are asked to write some thoughts about one specific coping skill they feel they have developed during their membership in the group.

Group Discussion:

The group leader encourages each member to elaborate about what he or she has written on each key holder. The group leader helps the member put these new coping skills into perspective.

Members are asked to interpret each other's responses, and explore whether or not they are now better equipped to deal with future difficulties. Members are often surprised at how positively others view their strengths and progress.

This exercise works well with groups well acquainted with each other, and is effective in the middle to later stages of group development.

NOTES

NOTES

NOTES

THE FOLLOWING PAGES CONTAIN:

1. Mailing list information

2. Information on other exciting group leader's guides

3. Information on possible multimedia editions of *Creative Therapy*

IF YOU FOUND THIS BOOK USEFUL . . .

You might want to know more about our other titles.

For a complete listing of our publications, please send us the following information. You may fold this sheet to make a postpaid reply envelope. (If you ordered this copy from Professional Resource Press [Professional Resource Exchange, Inc.], your name is already on our preferred customer mailing list.)

Name_____
(Please Print)

Address_____

Address_____

City/State/Zip_____

I am a _____ Psychologist; _____ Marriage and Family Therapist; _____ School Psychologist; _____ Clinical Social Worker; _____ Mental Health Counselor; _____ Psychiatrist; _____ Other:_____

Please fold on this line and the solid line below, tape (DO NOT STAPLE), and mail.

ADD A COLLEAGUE TO OUR MAILING LIST . . .

If you would like us to send our latest catalog to one of your colleagues, please return the form below:

Name_____
(Please Print)

Address_____

Address_____

City/State/Zip_____

This person is a _____ Psychologist; _____ Marriage and Family Therapist; _____ School Psychologist; _____ Clinical Social Worker; _____ Mental Health Counselor; _____ Psychiatrist; _____ Other:_____

THANK YOU!

Please fold on this line and the solid line above, tape (DO NOT STAPLE), and mail.

Please cut along dotted line, fold along solid lines, and tape.

3 OTHER EXCITING TITLES FOR GROUP LEADERS . . .

STRUCTURED ADOLESCENT PSYCHOTHERAPY GROUPS
Billie Farmer Corder

"A very welcome addition to the mental health field because it provides a detached, clear model of group therapy written by a mental health professional with a vast amount of clinical experience leading therapy groups for diverse adolescent problems. This book is a gem, filled with outstanding practical and creative ways of engaging adolescents in the therapeutic group process. [The author's] extensive focus on the therapist's role as group leader is one of the important features of this book. The text is comprehensive yet concise in discussing methods of integrating adolescents with diverse cognitive, affective, and social skills and in structuring the group process to achieve expected therapeutic goals."
    -Cynthia R. Pfeffer, MD, Professor of Psychiatry, Cornell University Medical College;
    Chief, Child Psychiatry Inpatient Unit, The NY Hospital - Westchester Division

A "must read" book if you are a therapist who works with adolescents and their families. Contains how-to-do-it guidelines for each step in forming and leading a group including client selection and evaluation, goal setting, evaluating group process, relationships with a co-therapist, and much more.

Provides specific techniques for use in the beginning, middle, and end phases of time-limited structured psychotherapy groups. Offers concrete suggestions for working with "hard to reach" and difficult adolescents, providing feedback to parents, and dealing with administrative, legal, and ethical issues. Includes immediately usable examples of pre-/post-evaluation forms, therapy contracts, evaluation feedback letters, parent response forms, therapist rating scales, co-therapist rating forms, problem identification forms, supervision and session records, client and parent handouts, and specific group exercises. This book is solidly anchored to research on the curative factors in group therapy and includes empirical data, numerous references, theoretical formulations, and examples of group sessions.

◆ ◆ ◆

THERAPEUTIC EXERCISES FOR VICTIMIZED & NEGLECTED GIRLS:
Applications for Individual, Family, & Group Psychotherapy
Pearl Berman

". . . must reading for anyone who wants to help children heal the wounds from the violence they have experienced. Berman has given therapists just the right combination of supportive therapy with empathy together with action exercises that address the content areas most therapists miss. It's a program that can easily be used by students as well as the most experienced clinician."
    -Lenore E. Walker, EdD, ABPP, Denver, Colorado

The author presents 27 structured and focused therapeutic exercises designed to improve the effectiveness of your work with victimized and neglected girls in individual, group, and family therapy. Offers specific guidelines for selecting and implementing exercises focused on the specific needs of individual clients. Contains numerous case examples and therapist resources. Also includes a client handbook that you can photocopy and distribute to reinforce the concepts and skills covered in the exercises.

Skill-building exercises are presented, with full instructions, for recognizing and identifying feelings; developing assertive communication and problem-solving skills; improving peer and parental relationships; and recognizing, understanding, and dealing with sexuality, physical victimization, and sexual victimization. Printed in an 8-1/2" X 11" format.

◆ ◆ ◆

STRESS MANAGEMENT TRAINING:
A Group Leader's Guide
Nancy Norvell and Dale Belles

"The authors outline in detail the elements of a comprehensive approach to stress management and demonstrate their clinical expertise through providing examples of how such a program can be implemented in actual practice and how it can be employed with diverse occupational groups. . . . It represents a significant contribution to the clinical stress management literature.
    -James H. Johnson, PhD, Professor, Department of Clinical and Health Psychology,
    College of Health Related Professions, University of Florida

This practical guide will help you define the concept of stress for group members and teach them various intervention techniques ranging from relaxation training to communication skills. Includes specific exercises, visual aids, stress response index, stress analysis form, and surveys for evaluating program effectiveness. Clinicians can easily modify these techniques for use with individual clients.

PRICES AND ORDER FORM ON REVERSE SIDE

Please Send Me:

_____ Copies of *Structured Adolescent Psychotherapy Groups*
(List Price: $19.95 each. Please add shipping noted below.*)

_____ Copies of *Therapeutic Exercises for Victimized & Neglected Girls*
(List Price: $24.95 each. Please add shipping noted below.*)

_____ Copies of *Stress Management Training: A Group Leader's Guide*
(List Price: $12.95 each. Please add shipping noted below.*)

*Shipping Charges
Up to $14.99 Order, Add $2.75 in US, $4.75 Foreign
$15 to $29.99 Order, Add $3.25 in US, $5.25 Foreign
$30 to $44.99 Order, Add $3.75 in US, $5.75 Foreign
$45 to $59.99 Order, Add $4.25 in US, $6.25 Foreign
Orders over $60, Add 7% in US, 10% Foreign
(Call for charges for 1, 2, or 3 day US delivery or Foreign air)

All orders from individuals and private institutions must be prepaid in full. Florida residents, add 7% sales tax. Prices and availability subject to change without notice.

For fastest service (purchase and credit card orders only)
CALL TOLL FREE 1-800-443-3364
Weekdays 9:00 - 5:00 Eastern Time
or
FAX 1-813-366-7971
24 hours a day

Check or money order enclosed (US funds only) $_____

Charge my (circle):   Visa   MasterCard   American Express   Discover

Card #_____

Exp. Date_____   Daytime Phone # (_____)_____

Signature_____

Please fold on this line and the solid line below, tape (DO NOT STAPLE), and mail.

❒   Order enclosed (ship to name and address below).

❒   Please add my name to your mailing list and send me your latest catalog. (If you ordered this copy from Professional Resource Press [Professional Resource Exchange, Inc.], your name is already on our Preferred Customer Mailing List.)

Name_____
(Please Print)

Address_____

Address_____

City/State/Zip_____

I am a _____ Psychologist; _____ Clinical Social Worker; _____ Marriage and Family Therapist; _____ Mental Health Counselor; _____ School Psychologist; _____ Psychiatrist; _____ Other: _____

THANK YOU!

Please fold on this line and the solid line above, tape (DO NOT STAPLE), and mail.

BUSINESS REPLY MAIL FIRST-CLASS MAIL PERMIT NO 445 SARASOTA FL	**NO POSTAGE NECESSARY IF MAILED IN THE UNITED STATES**

POSTAGE WILL BE PAID BY ADDRESSEE

PROFESSIONAL RESOURCE PRESS
PO BOX 15560
SARASOTA FL 34277-9900

Please cut along dotted line, fold along solid lines, and tape.

MULTIMEDIA EDITIONS OF *CREATIVE THERAPY*

We are considering developing Multimedia versions of the materials in the three *Creative Therapy* volumes for computer users who use Microsoft Windows. These Multimedia programs would offer numerous benefits in addition to the ability to view all text and illustrations on your computer screen. These would include:

- Instant access to specific exercises that are designed for groups in different stages of development.

- High speed searching for exercises with specified goals or criteria (e.g., encouraging self-disclosure).

- Immediate location of related exercises using "See also" hypertext links.

- On-demand printing of selected exercises and illustrations directly to your laser printer.

In order to use the Multimedia Editions of *Creative Therapy*, you will need to have the following minimum computer system (i.e., the programs will not be usable if these system requirements are not met):

An IBM compatible PC with an 80386 or higher processor.
4MB of RAM (8 MB recommended).
A hard disk with at least 7 MB of free space.
A VGA or SVGA color/monochrome monitor and graphics adapter.
Microsoft Windows operating system 3.1 or higher.
A Microsoft-compatible mouse, trackball, or other pointing device.
A laser printer that can print graphics using Microsoft Windows.
Optional: A 9600 baud (or faster modem) for express ordering and downloading of the program. The program would also be available on disk for mail delivery if you do not have a modem.

If you would like to receive more information on the Multimedia editions of *Creative Therapy* if we decide to develop these programs, please check the appropriate box on the reverse side of this page, and fold the page to form a prepaid envelope.

Now there are **THREE** Volumes of *Creative Therapy*!

Please send me:

_____ Copies of *Creative Therapy: 52 Exercises for Groups*
_____ Copies of *Creative Therapy II: 52 More Exercises for Groups*
_____ Copies of *Creative Therapy III: 52 More Exercises for Groups*
(List Price: $21.95 each. Please add shipping noted below.*)

*Shipping Charges
Up to $14.99 Order, Add $2.75 in US, $4.75 Foreign
$15 to $29.99 Order, Add $3.25 in US, $5.25 Foreign
$30 to $44.99 Order, Add $3.75 in US, $5.75 Foreign
$45 to $59.99 Order, Add $4.25 in US, $6.25 Foreign
Orders over $60, Add 7% in US, 10% Foreign
(Call for charges for 1, 2, or 3 day US delivery or Foreign air)

All orders from individuals and private institutions must be prepaid in full. Florida residents, add 7% sales tax. Prices and availability subject to change without notice.

For fastest service (purchase and credit card orders only)
CALL TOLL FREE 1-800-443-3364
Weekdays 9:00 - 5:00 Eastern Time
or
FAX 1-813-366-7971
24 hours a day

Check or money order enclosed (US funds only) $_____

Charge my (circle):   Visa   MasterCard   American Express   Discover

Card #_____

Exp. Date_____   Daytime Phone # (_____)_____

Signature_____

Please fold on this line and the solid line below, tape (DO NOT STAPLE), and mail.

❑   Order enclosed (ship to name and address below).
❑   Please add my name to your mailing list and send me your latest catalog. (If you ordered this copy from Professional Resource Press [Professional Resource Exchange, Inc.], your name is already on our Preferred Customer Mailing List.)
❑   I am interested in the Multimedia Windows Editions of *Creative Therapy*. Please send me more information if you develop this product. (Please read the description of the program and its basic system requirements on the back of this page.)

Name_____
                                         (Please Print)

Address_____

Address_____

City/State/Zip_____

I am a _____ Psychologist; _____ Clinical Social Worker; _____ Marriage and Family Therapist; _____ Mental Health Counselor; _____ School Psychologist; _____ Psychiatrist; _____ Other: _____

THANK YOU!

Please fold on this line and the solid line above, tape (DO NOT STAPLE), and mail.